I JUST WANT TO BE NORMAL

How to Overcome Problem Drinking & Be, Feel and Live Like A Social Drinker

This is the e-book version of I JUST WANT TO BE NORMAL-How to Overcome Problem Drinking & Be, Feel and Live Like A Social Drinker

The ReNova Method was developed by Michael O'Neal, LCDC-ADC III in collaboration with Mary Burgesser MD.

We hope you find it enlightening and helpful to you. It contains clear instructions on how the ReNova Method is performed and ways you can achieve this for yourself, with a counselor or with a series of download audio training recordings available to guide you.

We are available to help should you so desire. Reach out to us: https://renovarecoveryinstitute.com

Michael O'Neal, LCDC-ADC III Founder, ReNova Recovery Institute

"I Just Want To Be Normal"

Foreword

Can there really be a solution that turns alcoholics into social drinkers **_without_** the strange and often unbearable side effects of the Sinclair Method? Yes. That solution is the ReNova Method. It was discovered, as many advances have been, by accident. As the founder of DayRise Recovery my goal was to develop more effective sobriety-based treatments for alcohol and other drugs and in that we were successful. Far more of our clients achieved sobriety than the norm using 12 step approaches. But like all sobriety-based programs we had some failures. With our method however, we found that most of our clients who lapsed did so with far less drinking and emotional consequences. That is provided they kept using our methods.

At first my staff and I ignored the evidence of obvious 'harm reduction' in favor of our own pre-conceived ideas of what was the 'right' way to recover. But as the list of clients who experienced frequent but relatively minor lapses piled up, I found it impossible not to admit that something new and unexpected was happening. Still, the leap to trying for deliberate moderation was one of the most anguishing moments of my long career.

Could it be done with purpose? What would be the success rate both short and long term? What would be the failure rate? How could clients feel the vital sense of 'normalcy' and restoration if they kept drinking? I was to find the answers to these questions to be shocking. Yes, it could be done purposely, quite reliably it turned out. The short- and long-term success rate was better than with any sobriety-based approach I have ever seen, including our own. Clients not only achieved a sense of emotional 'normalcy' and restoration of self-esteem; they exceeded those who were practicing abstinence- in many *obvious* ways.

Ultimately it was found to be so powerfully effective that I completely changed my practice. I now devote myself and my resources full time to it exclusively. I changed the practice name as well, to match that of the method I developed. We are now ReNova Recovery Institute.

The Renova Recovery Method is the long hoped for process that really can help you go from problem drinker to normal drinker in just weeks. Each week you will see an improvement in your drinking until finally it will be within an entirely normal range. You will find other changes as well. Your restlessness will diminish, your mood and clarity of thought will increase. Sleep will improve.

So, why does ReNova succeed when so many other methods have failed? The answer is found in the old fable about the five blind men and the elephant. As you will recall, each of the five felt a different part of the elephant and came to very separate conclusions. That is what has happened with prior approaches; each touched only part of the problem, while ReNova addresses drinking problems with a totally comprehensive 3:1 approach of pharmacotherapy, neurotherapy and self-induced mind therapy. Eventually the first 2 elements become unneeded and the mind therapy alone will sustain the process. You will be completely independent and free of the effects of alcohol problems with that portion alone.

There is old saying that also applies; big things can come in small packages. ReNova Recovery Method is such a thing. It is compact. By that I mean it will not take up an extraordinary amount of time in helping you solve your drinking problem. A few hours a week will slowly give way to just 5-7 minutes a day as you progress with training.

Those few minutes will be among the best part of your day. You will come to look forward to them and feel better when you are done. Because of this they are naturally self-reinforcing. Those few simple minutes that you will come to enjoy will be helping you stay on a path that gives you consistent satisfaction through real control and restored pride.

Here is a message from I received recently a ReNova graduate who moved away to pursue his career. He sent it on the one-year anniversary of his training completion:

"Hey Mike;

I can't believe it's been a year. Well the drinking is splendid. I go many days in a a row without wanting to drink at all. When I do drink, I *rarely* have the desire to have more than 2-3 drinks. I still practice the relaxation almost daily. St. Patrick's was last night I had 4 beers which is the most I have had in one sitting for several weeks. Living _sober_ is very exciting."

Notice his last remark. To him, his drinking no longer even rises to a level beyond where he considers himself sober. When he began, he drank to black out frequently and well beyond reasonable almost every time. Now he drinks like most others, take it or leave, stop easily, enjoy it when he does drink. That is how normal people drink. That is how you can too with the help of ReNova.

What about complete abstinence? Can ReNova be used to achieve it? Yes, if that is your choice. Simply modify the mind training/visualization portion of the process to 'see' yourself happily abstaining. However, you may wish to try moderation first. See how it feels to at last be back in true control of your alcohol use and then assess if you want to go even further. You can achieve that on your own with proper study, preparation and effort. Further help is available should you desire-see 'How To get More Help' for details.

Why do I suggest moderation first? Because most people who try sobriety don't stay with it. Even using the ReNova Method the recovery rates is less than with our moderation program .

Here are some 'sobering' statistics on standard treatment:

According to research done by the pre-eminent psychiatrist James Dodes MD for his book "The Sober Truth" - Debunking the Bad Science Behind 12 Step Programs And The Rehab Industry:

Only 1/15 people who enter a 12-step program, the most common form of sobriety-based treatment, for alcohol recovery, is able to get and stay sober forever.

According to research conducted for the Journal of the American Medical Association (JAMA):

60% of alcoholics who undergo standard treatment and enter AA relapse within one year.

Clearly sobriety and the 12 step programs that support it are a huge failure.

ReNova Recovery Method applied to moderation produces much higher rates of success:

Nearly 6/7 persons who undergo the ReNova Method are still moderate at one year.

You will notice going forward that I use the term Alcohol Reaction Disorder or ARD except when describing cultural perceptions. The current Diagnostic and Statistical Manual of the American Psychiatric Association's preferred term of "Alcohol Use Disorder", while less pejorative than "Alcoholic" is still a behavioral (and subtle) blame label. It is also inconsistent with facts they themselves acknowledge. ARD is a brain disease caused by the brain's reaction to alcohol. A reaction that involuntarily occurs in a minority of persons who drink alcohol and is not a state they 'will' upon themselves.

How can anyone actually imagine that someone intentionally develops a drinking problem? That they voluntarily surrender control, face embarrassment, shame and fear, job loss, family loss, etc. on purpose? No one wakes up one day, at say at age 13, stretches and looks out the window while thinking to themselves "you know, when I grow up…I am gonna have a drinking problem, yeah that's a great idea!" It is well past time that we stop blaming people for something they had no idea would happen, no idea it is happening and can only see has happened when it is too late to change it.

The world will be a better place when we do. Far more people will seek help when they understand that what is wrong is happening to them, not because of them. This is especially true when they know they can have a normal life that does not include the need to deprive them self of a commonly used pleasure, one their friends and family members freely enjoy at their will.

You will also notice that this book is intentionally written in laymen's terms to as great degree as possible. This book is about helping and the clearer the instructions the better.

Chapter One

Feelings About Alcohol

From the moment man 1st crushed grapes, alcohol has played an enormous role in human history. Medicine, religious ceremonies, celebration, seduction and romance, relaxation… and hell on earth despair. Our feelings as a species, about alcohol, are as mixed as the practices in which it is used and the results it produces.

Poems, sonnets and songs without number have been composed about its use. One iconic Country & Western song included the brag that, because (in part) it included, "gettin' drunk", it was now the perfect Country& Western song.

Movies, television shows and radio broadcasts constantly show and/or talk about alcohol in terms glowing and glowering.

Television ads and billboards clutter our minds to the point of conscious non perception portraying it as an essential element of sex, glamour and the good life.

Stroll through any market in most areas of the world and you find it embedded in displays next to breads, meats and other drinks.

Attend any Sunday Mass and find a priest performing the 'mystery' of transforming it in the blood of Jesus Christ.

Attend a Southern Baptist Revival and hear it reviled as an evil trap… for wicked sinners. Jokes about those same ministers drinking in secret? Too numerous to include here.

The spouse who demands the 'right' to keep a bottle in the refrigerator because they shouldn't have to "be deprived" is the same one who will threaten divorce if their loved one has one more lapse to alcohol.

People headed into a liquor store will have a mixture of pity and disgust at the advanced ARD victim standing near the door panhandling for enough money to get some for himself.

One of the most popular TV shows in history was about a bar and its regular patrons with 'the gangs all here' warmth and certain characters having designated stools. Another iconic show featured a man who would lock himself up in the small town jail each time he got drunk. The next day he would take the keys out of the hands of the hapless deputy to let himself out; now sober. The deputy and the drunk acting as if it was all perfectly normal. "See ya next time Otis" the usual departing line from the deputy. The drunk treated as if he were a regular breakfast customer at the local cafe.

Priests and physicians have (historically) been held in high regard, their use of alcohol, seen for different reasons, as a blessing.

From most, the college "party animal" is looked at with an indulgence equal to the enormous amount consumed during these 'rites of passage'.

In many countries alcohol is a ubiquitous part of sport events. Drinking during 'tail gates' and in the stands is not even remarked upon.

The professional who comes home and has 'a double' before dinner is a well-known archetype and usually well tolerated by family.

None think it scandalous or bizarre that Queen Elizabeth II, now in her nineties, still has 2 Gin & Du-bonnet's every day at noon and champagne every night.

The hard-driven sales person, who drinks just as hard, is usually 'put up' with by their firm and family.

And near the bottom of the rung of human society, in terms of regard, are those seen to not to use alcohol within societies expected norms. Even one the official definitions of Alcohol Reaction Disorder frames 'alcoholism' in terms of being irresponsible rather than the amount consumed, when or why. "Continued use of alcohol despite knowledge of adverse consequences"

All of these conflicted feelings about alcohol, those who use it and the results they get from it, form a powerful daily message that becomes silently ingrained in our collective minds. Love the alcohol and hate the alcoholic.

Chapter Two

Alcohol Does Not Cause Alcoholism

Drink 8 glasses of water a day. We all here that advice, given for our good health. But you wouldn't have heard it in 17th century London. The people there were rightly afraid to drink the water. Drinking the water could cause deadly disease. So, people of that time believed drinking water, in and of itself, was bad for you. To them it was a clear case of cause and effect: drink water, get sick, maybe die = water is bad for you. Instead everyone of any age beyond young childhood commonly drank beer, ale and wine. It wasn't the water of course; it was the contaminating bacteria. Bacteria they rid themselves of by boiling the water for the beer they consumed in its place. Had you told them that, they likely would have laughed at you or turned you into the authorities on suspicion of witchcraft?

People from the dawn of time believed that the sun rotated around the earth from below to above. They could see each morning that the sun 'rising' in the east and each night it 'set' in the west. To them it was a clear case of cause and effect: see the sun 'coming up' see the sun 'going down'= equals the sun revolves around the earth. If you had told them that the earth is a (semi) round globe that turns in a 24-hour rotation they would have thought you either insane or a heretic.

Thanks to the likes of Lister, Copernicus and Galileo, the modern world has long ago set aside these incorrect cause and effect perceptions and no serious (and sane) person believes these things anymore.

An endless list of such wrong cause and effect beliefs could be offered, but let us focus on the one at hand. Alcohol does not cause alcoholism.

A few rough statistics to cite:

87% of adults in America have consumed alcohol in their lifetimes

52% have consumed alcohol in the last 30 days

30 percent have consumed more than a drink this week

10% have consumed more than 10 drinks today

So, if alcohol is the actual cause of alcoholism why don't we have a population in which at least 30% if not 52% or 87% of adults are alcoholics? That would be clear cause and effect wouldn't it? Drink alcohol, become addicted to alcohol. But it doesn't work that way does it?

Now, think for a moment about another drug: nicotine. It has a reputation for being highly addictive doesn't it? Yet, how many people have you known who smoke (or these days vape) only when they are drinking alcohol? If such a person goes for days or even weeks without drinking, they also go days or weeks without nicotine. How can that be, if when they do drink several times in a week they also smoke/vape?

The fact is that even the most 'addictive drug' isn't always addictive. So, obviously it isn't the drug, whether it is alcohol, nicotine or something else…even opiates. It is how our brains react to those substances.

That's why fixing the real problem, is the real solution to 'alcoholism'. It doesn't require abstaining to do that, it just requires fixing the brain reactions. That includes brain chemistry reaction, anxiety, depression & insomnia reaction and emotionally stored self-perception reaction. Unless all of that is fixed at the same time, ultimately things stay the same and people remain vulnerable to out-of-control drinking, no matter how long they abstain. That is why ReNova works, because it 'fixes' all of these things at the same time and you can then drink normally e.g. without adverse reactions including the compulsion to keep drinking beyond a reasonable limit.

Chapter Three

Which Disease?

24 years ago, I had the extraordinary luck to be hired at Summer Sky Treatment Center, one of the best, and at the time, few remaining 28-day treatment centers. During the

1990's insurance companies had cut reimbursements to the bone for addiction treatment and length of stay elsewhere had shrunk to an average of 10 days inpatient. It wasn't that 'the Sky' as we called it, was doing any better with insurance companies. It was the fact that the owner was a wealthy woman who cared more about helping than making money. This remarkable woman, named Cathern Brooks, had opened Summer Sky long after most others had retired. A tiny and perceptive spitfire Cathern ruled 'the Sky' with a gnarled iron fist. About 1:3 treatment episodes were done entirely free and it was common for us to invite nearly everyone to stay an additional week on top of the 28 days. Only those unfamiliar with the treatment industry would wonder why I take the space to note these facts*. Cathern became a life-long hero and example to me.

Cathern was however much more than a hero to me; she was my advocate when others sought to restrain me, which happened a lot. She allowed me a remarkably wide berth that she afforded few others and I did my best to be worthy of her trust. A year into my employment I was made the family counselor. My job was to conduct weekend education and healing experiences for those who were willing to participate in their loved one's recovery.

I inherited the program from my mentor, the late Bill Harris under who I had studied at Institute For Addictions, one of the best proprietary schools in the country for addiction counselors. Tragically Bill had a severe car accident and couldn't continue in either position.

His program at the Sky was the standard fare of the day: Some facts about addiction, as understood at the time, followed by family 'confrontation'. This was a kind of '2-men enter, 1-man leaves' experience in which family members vented their anger and other feelings to their loved one in treatment.

That no one else had noticed (or correlated) the high "against medical advice" departure rate of patients within 2 days of this experience was remarkable to me. But I was determined to do something about it.

Facing down Al Conlin, the facility's renowned Executive Director* I insisted on changing the Family Program entirely. Cathern once again backed me up, despite the hard feelings it caused, and a new approach was born.

That approach was to emphasize healing in a subtle way through education about addiction and to seek to re-bond the family to the patient while giving them some things they needed beyond knowledge:

A role that allowed them to be useful in recovery and avoided labeling them as "enablers"

Reassurance that they were "normal"

By the latter I mean all of their pent of feelings and fears were normal. The technique I used to get them to understand that was simple. After some ice breaking basic Q&A about the facility and rules, and some basic discussion about what they had experienced etc., I drew a line from top to bottom in the middle of a white board that sat on the stage of the old church where the family program was conducted. On one side I wrote the word "Normal" and on the other side I wrote the word "Abby". I then explained that "Abby" was taken from an old movie "Young Frankenstein" and recounted the amusing scenario between Gene Wilder and Marty Feldman that relates to the name i.e. "Abby Normal, yes I'm almost sure that was the name". Once I had them relaxed and loosened up that way, I then began to pose questions to them like:

"Is it normal or Abby to be happy that your loved one comes home broke after a weekend binge?"

"Is it normal or Abby to feel embarrassed when your husband, dead drunk calls your dad at tight as—d bastard at Thanksgiving?"

I would get them to answer out loud as a group and then write the questions on the correct side of the board until both sides were full. Then I would step off the stage, walk up to them and in a quiet reassuring tone say "OK…so you're normal" I always got a lot of reaction to that moment. Laughter, tears, clapping etc.

Once we finished processing that we moved on to the next important item, getting them to see their loved one in a new light that would make reconciliation easier to achieve.

I would write "the name of a disease" as I told them on a piece of paper. Then I would seal it in an envelope and hand it to the most dominant (and usually angry) male in the audience of attendees who seemed to have formed at least some alliance with me through the time we had spent so far.

Then turning back to the white-board I would write the following:

Causes gross distortion of judgment and thinking.

Overwhelming bad smell in your breath.

Can result in coma or death

Causes intense craving

Life-long chronic condition

Can result in multiple hospitalizations

Car crashes and accidents can be a result

Many organs affected

Men can become impotent especially at peak moments of condition

Wasn't thought of as 'real' disease until the 20th century

I would then ask the audience to name the disease. Suspecting a trick question, they usually paused.

The Answer? Diabetes.

Usually, I had to have the man open the envelope and read it aloud. A hush often came over the attendees as most just stared at the board thinking and struggling to accept the similarities.

Read the list above again. Pay attention to your emotional reactions. Disbelief, discounting?

That is because we are conditioned to discount the suffering of the alcoholic and blame instead.

But, consider this: The same was once true of diabetic men until the mid-20th century. Diabetes used to be considered a "woman's condition." Families would cover up the condition if a man had it, as it was considered deeply shameful. That was before insulin was available which changed the landscape of public perception.

Just as left handed people were until recently considered mentally deficient. King George VI, the father of Queen Elizabeth was so traumatized by the brutal attempts to 're-educate' him to use his right hand that he developed a life-long stammer, memorialized in a recent popular film.

The point of course is that there are many things we are culturally 'trained' to believe that are not true just as I noted in the preceding chapter 'Alcohol Does Not Cause Alcoholism.'

Here is a truth:

Diabetes and alcoholism are both involuntarily acquired diseases whose origins are biological in nature and manifest many of the same symptoms and consequences.

Now ask yourself a question, would you tell a diabetic to 'snap out of it' get their act together and feel disgusted if they didn't stop having the symptoms of diabetes?

"Of course not, that would be ridiculous, diabetes is a disease" was your immediate answer ... wasn't it?

*Under the leadership of Scott Kelley the fine legacy of Summer Sky's clinical program continues. I have referred many to it who want a more 12 step-based solution.

**Al Conlin was the man responsible for Texas being the 1st state to actually license chemical dependency counselors, clearing the way for insurance reimbursement for our work outside of treatment facilities and setting an example for that many other states have followed.

Chapter 4

The Five Types of 'Alcoholics'

There are 5 sub types of diabetes that range in severity from mild to extreme. There are 5 subtypes of ARD that range in severity from mild to extreme.

<u>Alpha type.</u> This sub type is not physiologically dependent upon alcohol. Drinking is usually in the mildly to moderately heavy range of consumption. This subtype is typically able to control consumption to a limited degree, especially when outside factors discourage use in circumstances. Nevertheless, daily heavy drinking will lead in most cases to more advanced stages of alcoholism.

<u>Beta type.</u> This sub type is also not physiologically dependent upon alcohol, but usually drinks quite heavily. Often, doing so to the point of intoxication induced unconsciousness (passing out). This sub type may have physical difficulties related alcohol use via due to heavy drinking. Moderation can help reverse this damage, or at the very least, may prevent it from becoming worse.

<u>Gamma type.</u> This sub type is physiologically dependent and is typically unable to demonstrate any control over consumption on routine basis. This sub type is the one most classically associated with people's minds with alcohol reaction disorder. Provided extensive neurological damage, such as Korsakoff/Wernicke's Encephalopathy, is not a factor, this sub type can successfully moderate with ReNova.

<u>Delta type.</u> Similar to Gamma type this individual sub type drinks on a continuous basis and heavily. However, this type is most clearly characterized by the inability to abstain as opposed to the inability to stop, even when sufficient reasons are present.

<u>Epsilon type.</u> This is, somewhat idiosyncratically, referred to as the most advanced type of alcohol reaction disorder. Individuals with the sub type of alcohol problems do not drink on a routine basis. For this reason, they are referred to in layman's terms as periodic alcoholic. Epsilon types are the rarest among the five sub types. They are also the sub type least likely to seek help for alcohol reaction disorder, because of the infrequency of their drinking. However, when consuming alcohol this sub type nearly universally experiences chemical induced amnesia (blackouts) and can function in an anti- social manner, such as assaults, driving under the influence and other phenomena that would be anathema to their normal behavior. Moderation is possible for the sub type however, our normal suggestions, which include gradual

discontinuance of medication, upon medical advice, should be revised to include continuous low dose use of Naltrexone.

Chapter 5

How the Brain Works In ARD Victims

As noted above ARD is a brain disease. It manifests as a complex neuro-psycho-social disorder. In order to understand ARD it is important to know the basics of how it affects the brain. There are three areas of the brain that are chiefly affected. The same three areas are addressed by ReNova…that is why it works. Those three areas are:

The Mesolimbic System.

This area of our brains makes and/or causes the release of our neurochemistry. Brain chemistry, or neurotransmitters, are the chemical messengers that prompt actions and regulate emotions. Dopamine, GABA, Endorphins and Serotonin all play key roles in prompting a wide range of actions and reactions in human life. The brain's balance of these messengers are key determinates of success in controlling alcohol use and many other things.

The Amygdala.

This part of the brain has long been known by scientists for its ability to prompt anxious reactions. Perhaps as a vehicle for our survival, it stores and uses information to help us feel threat. Modern threat, however, is rarely about immediate survival. It is more subtle and complex and continuous. That maybe one of the reasons ARD is more common in our modern world than was known to exist in traditional tribal societies.

The frontal and pre-frontal lobes of the brain.

The last and most fragile part of our brains to develop, it helps us think in complex terms; language, mathematics, science, religion/morality, and self-image/self-perception. One of the functions of this area of the brain is to help us control impulses and to reason out why we take certain actions.

So, working together it goes something like this in ARD:

The Mesolimbic system prompts us to do something to manufacture more of its desired chemicals.

The Amygdala prompts us to feels a sense of vague threat or unease.

The Frontal Lobes conclude something like "OK, I'm gonna have a drink to relax, loosen up (response to prompts from mesolimbic and amygdala) but, I'm gonna stop at one or two." (Reason, morality).

Sometimes with ARD, through will power and/or circumstance, such as a loved one's displeasure, that works. We might even feel a sense of pride or relief that we did it. But, not a real sense of satisfaction. Why? Because the brain chemistry system didn't get its fill and it is left 'hungry'. Then, of course, there are those other times when it does get full expression of its desires.

How do we feel at such moments, especially if something bad happens or we experience reproach from a loved one or friend? Remorse, guilt, shame, depression, a sense of defeat and self-disappointment are common reactions.

Repeat that often enough and self-image starts to take a hit. We begin to see ourselves in a negative light and begin to apply negative self-talk along with strong admonishment to 'do better the next time.' But as the neurochemical systems demands grow and the sense of vague threat gets greater, our brains governance gets gradually less and less effective and self-image gets worse and worse. So, by the time someone has to deal with a drinking problem self-esteem is usually very low no matter what else they may have accomplished in their lives and/or whatever other aspects of their character are of high social value when sober (see chapter "Dr. Jekyll, May I Introduce Mr. Hyde).

That is why even the use of modern medications that suppress the desire to drink are not usually successful. They address only one part of a now very complex problem. Even when combined with counseling they still don't address the 3rd key area, the amygdala and its ability to prompt a stream of vague feelings of threat. I have seen many persons using standard 12 step approaches and pharmaco-therapy combinations display restlessness, hypersensitivity, obsessive behaviors and impulsive actions for years into 'recovery'. Are their lives better than when they were drinking? Certainly, but they are far from complete. ReNova can give a complete life that includes the perfectly normal and common pleasure of having a drink or two, enjoying it and being fully able to stop while feeling genuinely satisfied.

Chapter 6

A Brief History of Some Other Solutions

A William Rudd

A doctor who signed the Declaration of Independence, Rudd was well ahead of his time. He wrote of his (correct) belief that inebriates, as they were described in his day, were suffering from an illness. Before and after his time alcohol problems have been (mostly) dealt with by futile punishment. The stockades of the Puritans, for example, are images burned into the consciousness of virtually everyone. Punishment, however, is not a deterrent in most cases. It never has been, it never will be. Why? Because, you simply cannot punish an illness into being good… no matter how hard you try.

Fortunately, more enlightened methods have been tried as well. A generation beyond Rudd came the 1st real effort to deal with the problem.

The Washingtonians

A group called the Washingtonians was formed in 1840. Four friends in a Baltimore tavern pledged to help one another to stop drinking. This gave birth to a movement that spread quickly. In a few years' time, The Washingtonians had an estimated membership in the hundreds of thousands. Considering the population of the United States was 8 million in the 1840's their membership comparatively dwarfed that of AA today. The term 'taking the pledge' was borrowed by the Temperance movement from The Washingtonians. The relative success of the approach (swear off and stick together) cannot be fairly judged from this distance in time. What is certain is that The Washingtonians did not last long. By the end of the 1840's they had dwindled. Apparently this was through in fighting regarding the Temperance Movement and Abolition. The movement was so forgotten that Bill Wilson, the founder of AA, claimed to have no knowledge of them when a hundred years later he formed Alcoholics Anonymous.

The Temperance Movement

 The Temperance Movement began to be prominent in 1820. The Movement sought to ban alcohol altogether seeing it as the cause of human suffering foisted upon man by evil influences. It finally succeeded with the passage of the 18th amendment to the US constitution. Prohibition, as it came to be called, lasted 13 years from 1920-1933. Its lasting chief effect was the birth of modern organized crime. Most drinking Americans of the day refused to stop drinking. The 'speak easy' culture of the 1920's just criminalized the activity of millions every day.

Alcoholics Anonymous

AA is the most influential self-help movement in history it was formally born on June 10 th, 1935. AA has had multi-millions of members over the years around the globe. It claims in its literature that anyone can succeed at their program if they are honest and are diligent enough in their efforts. That portion of the text is read aloud at virtually all meetings held of the organization. While calling them 'suggestions' the clear implication is: you must work the steps and have a spiritual awakening in order to 'make it' in sobriety. This involves getting a more senior member to 'sponsor' you e.g. serve as your adviser with the steps and in life. It also claims to be a spiritual not religious program and is all volunteer, no one profits.

It has spawned numerous self-help groups for other issues like drugs, overeating, gambling and sexual addiction. Professionals with advanced degrees and treatment centers everywhere use and endorse their approach.

While declining to provide any evidence of its own, AA has nourished a reputation of being broadly effective.

It began with Bill Wilson, AA founder and guider-in-chief during his lifetime. Wilson was a shrewd promoter who built AA from just a few members to very nearly a half million consistent attendees by his death in 1970. He carefully built his own reputation as well and is considered by many in AA as benign type of patron saint.

He is portrayed as giving and selfless and sober to the day of his death.

But does all of this compare to reality?

In addition to the statistics cited in the Foreword:

In 2014 the Substance Abuse and Mental Health Services Administration (SAMHSA) conducted an in depth survey. It found that 48% of *people attending an AA meeting had less than 30 days of sobriety*.

Also in the 1990's the National Association of Alcohol & Drug Abuse Counselors released findings that showed people go through treatment 6 times in a lifespan.

Suicide is a shockingly frequent cause of death among AA members.

Sexual exploitation of new members is so common it has a euphemism "13th Stepping"

AA general service board members earn six figure salaries for part time work.

As to Wilson himself the reality is also far different from the projection. AA's basic text, nicknamed 'the Big Book" had 32 different authors. But Wilson alone obtained the copyright and earned royalties off its sales the remainder of his life, constantly promising a portion that never came to the others. The large home he lived in was paid for and maintained by AA. The famous 12 steps were plagiarized from the 6 tenants of the Oxford Groups where Wilson originally sober up. He never acknowledged this, but a side by side comparison makes it starkly obvious.

While claiming fidelity to his wife in his writings, he was in fact a prolific serial womanizer.

As to Wilson's 'continuous sobriety' that too depends on twisting perspective. Doesn't LSD count? Wilson is known to have used the drug many times. Barbiturates have also been reported.

For all of the above, it is also true that AA has no doubt benefited many who have tried it, albeit a minority have achieved stable long-term sobriety.

So is AA a mutual self-help society that has benefited many, or a cult-like organization that succeeds long term with a minority, exploits the vulnerable and serves a tiny group at the top with undeserved and secretive monies? The answer is-Yes.

And what about Wilson himself? A true helper, or a hypocrite, con artist and thief? Perhaps his final acts are the most revealing ones:

Those present with him admit he died begging for a drink.

He left his royalty rights in his will to his wife…and final his mistress. Nothing for the surviving fellow writers.

Full disclosure: This writer was a member of AA for 30 years. I was sober throughout those 30 years. I never worked 'the steps' and I didn't attend AA meetings daily as so many do. In my opinion it is the constant immersion that causes most to stay sober. Statements repeated as mantras by members like "meeting makers make it", "Keep coming back", "if you don't come to meetings, you hear what happens to people who don't come to meetings" etc. foster that cult like dependence. It is a dependence that can consume much of member's non-working life, and leads to deep imbalances, family strains and many other problems.

William Rogers and Kenneth Blum of the University of Texas

In the 1950's and again in the 1980's research scientists at the University of Texas made critical breakthroughs in understanding the role that the building blocks of neurotransmitters play in controlling levels of addiction to alcohol and other substances. Rogers and his team in the 1950's found that a key amino acid, L-Glutamine was somewhat successful in reducing drinking in persons with Alcohol Problems. One generation later Kenneth Blum re validated this and found amino acids also play a role in helping with a wide variety of drug abuse.

Enriched levels of these amino acids helped control the 'hunger' for a drug (different amino acid combinations affect different drug hunger and different sub types of ARD victims require different combinations). The tragedy of these discoveries being essentially ignored is not hard to understand. You cannot patent an amino acid, they are naturally occurring compounds.

Still, a small but growing amount of treatment facilities use the knowledge to help their clients. Much of the 'holistic' trend in treatment is based on these findings.

DayRise Recovery, which I founded in 2005, was among these centers. Eventually this knowledge formed a one part of the ReNova Alcohol Protocol.

The Schick/Schadel Method

Popular in the 1960s through the 1980s this method sought to use a Pavlovian kind of conditioned response. Confined in a hospital setting alcoholics were exposed to a powerfully undesirable response, drink alcohol/vomit-repeatedly. This 'therapy' was done for period of two week or more twice every day. Short term success appears to have been high, long term success not so much.

Dangerous and cruel this method faded. Once nationwide they are reduced to a single facility that practices a variation of the approach.

Antabuse

Similar in effect to Schick/Schadel this medication serves as a deterrent to drinking. Physically violent reactions, that are potentially fatal, occur if alcohol is consumed after taking this medication. Many with ARD, however, learn to drink despite the medication. The very fact they do so is an indication that their brain's survival mechanism has, in the words of the National Institute on Drug Abuse, been hijacked and perverted. This medication is infrequently used today. When it is, that is mostly by local probation departments enforcing its use on people who have a history of relapse. It is unfortunately the only medication most people with a drinking disorder in the United States are aware exists.

The Sinclair Method

In 1962 a new medication was developed, Naltrexone. It did not become approved for alcohol use until the early 1990's. That did nothing to stop a brave and dedicated man, the American Psychologist John David Sinclair, from using it. He immigrated to Finland where his work and research would be more accepted and proceeded to have the 1st real medical, reliable, success with problem drinkers in history. Sinclair's approach was to shoot for 'pharmacological extinction' of drinking cues and cravings. His method was simple; he instructed patients to 'drink themselves sober' e.g. drink daily while taking the medication. Eventually the desire to drink at all, he believed, would fade to nothing. And it worked: for the minority who could tolerate the approach. The drawbacks to the Sinclair Method can be considerable: extreme nausea, loss of all sex drive, a dizzy or loopy feeling that can last for months, and slow results that can also take months. Still, something important happened among some of Sinclair's patients: sustained moderate drinking. In this manner the 1st successful option for moderation was born.

As you will read later in the book, a greatly reduced dose of Naltrexone is one of the support components in the ReNova Recovery Method. Our dosing recommendations are ***absent*** the undesirable side effects noted above.

Moderation Management

Founded with much fanfare in the early 1990's by a psychologist named Audra Kishline, the group banded together to control drinking using a group therapy format similar in some respects to AA. Being a behavioral based program, it rarely worked for heavy drinkers, including its founder. In a blackout, she struck a family with her car killing two children. In prison she persuaded Oprah Winfrey to interview her so she could repudiate her own work. Released, she changed her name and joined AA. Unable to stay sober she took her own life. The group itself survives in a diminished form, carefully encouraging heavy drinkers to look elsewhere for solutions.

Chapter 7

The ReNova Recovery Method

Why does the ReNova Recovery Method stand out from other approaches? There are 3 big reasons:

Consistent and quick efficacy. With ReNova not only are the results consistent, they come fast and build over a period of just weeks.

Lack of side effects. Unlike the Sinclair Method, ReNova rarely produces any side effects and when they occur, they are most often mild and very temporary.

Restored pride and sense of self-reliance. ReNova is something you will be taught to do, not something that will be forever done for you. Even the supports you will start with, will gradually give way. Much like a person going through physical rehabilitation gradually moves away from the need for coaches, props and technologies as they regain their own abilities.

Doing ReNova strictly on your own it will take longer to master unless you have previous experience with progressive relaxation and mental focus at deeper levels of consciousness.

If the above is the case, please note: you should NOT substitute any previous method you already know for this process. Instead simply allow your previous knowledge to be helpful in adapting to these new skills.

Written copies of the scripts are here for you to study.

When you do the exercises for yourself follow the 'script' for the mental component as exactly as possible. Read, and to the best of your ability, memorize them beforehand. This will be helped by visualizing the scenarios as you read them. Memorize only one at a time. Do the exercises in the exact sequence they are presented. Skipping ahead or leaving out any component is ill advised. Your goal with this is to get well. Imagine for a moment the results of an injured pro-athlete skipping parts of his/her physical rehab to hurry up and get back in the game. How would that work out do you suppose?

Chapter 8

Your Recovery Tool Kit

Like any repair job, certain tools will be needed to get the job done right.

It is best to learn about and gather these tools prior to starting. Understanding and familiarity with them will help the process be easier and success more assured.

<u>Naltrexone</u>

This is a prescription medication you can get from any doctor, physician assistant or advance practice nurse. Invented in 1962 at Menlo Laboratory it was originally hoped to be a replacement for morphine in the control of pain. The developers Blumberg, Dayton and Wolf found it was a complete failure in that sense. Instead of filling and soothing the brain's endorphin receptors as an opiate does, Naltrexone coats the receptor sites blocking endorphin transmitters from 'docking' in the receptors. Although a patent had been filed in 1963, no one appreciated the value of the drug at that time and it fell to complete disuse.

As noted above, American psychologist David Sinclair did see great value in the medication. He departed for Finland and began prescribing it for alcohol problems using his pharmacological extinction method to treat ARD (along with counseling of course). Although never admitted, it is likely that drug companies learned about his work and by 1992 the FDA allowed for its use with alcohol problems in the USA. At that time 12 step 'therapy' was still monolithic among treatment providers in America and prejudice against it prevented much wide spread prescription.

Naltrexone also seems equally effective in the treatment of opiate disorders with the limitation that an individual must be completely withdrawn from opiates before use of either oral or long acting naltrexone injections.

Still another use for naltrexone has been found. It is one of two ingredients in the now popular diet medication Contrave (™). In that medication a small dose of 8 mg. is combined with 90 mg. of bupropion hydrochloride, the generic of the anti-depressant medication Wellbutrin. The makers of Contrave encourage use of the medication for 3 months before results should be evaluated because of the building up effectiveness of the drug.

Patients at the ReNova Recovery Institute are also prescribed a small dose (12.5 mg), combined with the lowest possible dose of bupropion hydro-chloride (75 mg). and it is advised to be used along with key amino acids and herbs in separate formula we developed. Just as with Contrave, a gradual build up effect is experienced with this dose of naltrexone/bupropion combination. Buildup it is faster however with our combination and the aminos; about 30 days to marked reduction. This helps in the creation of the conditioned response. Note we have found the 8mg dose to low to be effective for ReNova. *So, getting a prescription for Contrave to use for ReNova is not advisable.*

Bupropion

This medication is a dopamine re-uptake inhibitor. It is commonly prescribed for depression, smoking cessation and attention deficit disorder. It should not be mixed with any other anti-depressants except on the advice of your medical doctor.

Like Naltrexone, Bupropion has been used for a longtime, has a good safety record and any side effects are mild and well tolerated by most people.

Your training will gradually take over so that will help you stay permanently stable without these medications but _they are essential in the beginning_.

Three others things to note about the 12.5 mg and bupropion 75 mg doses:

As discussed previously, virtually no side effects are ever felt and they are mild and short term if they occur.

Patients consistently report a greater sense of pleasure from alcohol without a corresponding increased sense of intoxication. This is the exact opposite of what is experienced with high dose Naltrexone used in the Sinclair Method. We believe this to be the result of combining it with Bupropion, because that medication is a dopamine re uptake inhibitor. The combination may cause a steady, but lower flow and availability of dopamine. Without an overabundance of dopamine, perception may be increased and lower alcohol use also causes less distortion.

These doses may be the reason for decreased tolerance for alcohol experienced by our patients. This lower tolerance also helps reduce the amount of alcohol consumed. This seems to occur even among ARD victims who have begun with the familiar high tolerance seen in genetically vulnerable people.

Again, we have no firm explanation for this result and further research of the type best conducted in a large scale study involving sophisticated methodologies and pharmaco-genetic testing would be needed to provide one. What is obvious is that the small size of the dose, the speed with which it happens, the frequency of occurrence across the entire age and health range etc. indicates the result is no way related to potential cause of concern related to alcohol metabolism.

Nutritional supplements

One of the reasons ARD is usually progressive is that the store of brain chemicals become depleted through over stimulation. In order to rebuild the supply, you need their basic building blocks; key components of the branch chain amino acids found in proteins. These nutrients are similar in effect to vitamins. You will need at least two key vitamins as well, B1 and B6, as well as some specific amino acids. Brake, by the ReNova Institute is the most complete formula available and can be purchased by contacting us at https://renovarecoveryinstitute.com. Brake supports the Naltrexone/Bupropion and allows the smaller doses to be the most effective.

Other commercial made options are available. In my view, there is very little difference between them all except the price. A one-month supply costing between

$99.00 and $250.00 for essentially the same ingredients in each of them and all far less complete than Brake. These formulas can be purchased on Amazon or directly from the makers.

CES Neurostimulators

CES Ultra or Alpha-Stim. (Either device, not both) These are _gentle_ prescription neurostimulators that help the brain re balance itself by apparently calming the Amygdala. They are FDA approved for the treatment of anxiety, depression and insomnia. Any licensed healthcare provider, including licensed counselors and therapists can prescribe their use. Until recently most healthcare providers were unaware of these powerfully useful tools. That began to change when the Veterans Administration started use of Alpha-Stim in its programs, including its substance abuse programs. Still you may find physicians and therapists who either haven't heard of them or know little about them.

You can download a prescription forms from either of their manufacturer's websites. A consultation is also available through our website to get a CES Ultra. CES Ultra is half the price of Alpha-Stim ($379.00 v. $750.00) and there was no difference seen in outcomes among our clients.

A strong word of caution here. There are quite a few imitators out there including a knock off Chinese machine called CES Alpha-Stim. You don't need a prescription for the knock off so it may be tempting. _The exact patented stimulation strength is important for success and only CES Ultra and Alpha Stim have it_. A huge number of peer reviewed studies are available for review on these devices and their effect on brain health. Get the real deals here, they are worth it.

Also beware that devices that claim a direct effect on addiction are out there. Studies show that these un-prescribed 'brain stimulators might help temporarily but can have a BIG boomerang effect later. Again, you are in this to win, so make the right choice here.

Chapter 9

Developing a Commitment Mindset

ReNova will not cure you of ARD*, instead it will teach you how to manage it, so you can have a normal life. A life where you are genuinely free to feel and behave and choose just like everyone else who is healthy in a psychological sense and does not feel compelled to keep drinking alcohol beyond a reasonable limit.

It will also help you 'fix' the anger you may feel at yourself for having ARD and will give you a tool to prompt ongoing self-management to prevent regression.

But conscious choice and mind set are important too, not just the 'tool' to prompt ongoing effort. So, I'm going to ask you now to do something before you begin your process of fixing your drinking. This is something that is designed to help cement a conscious choice to keep with it, from the start and years from now as well.

I'm going to ask you to write out two life scenarios. One, where you stop using the tools, or, at least stop being consistent with them. The other, where you stay with the tools as long as needed and the self-regulation therapy on a daily basis from this point forward.

You don't have to go into great detail with long narrative, although you can, they're your stories after all. But, make them long enough to include what you think will really happen in both scenarios. Don't put a lot of 'thought' into them, or focus on grammar and spelling. Let them be streams of consciousness.

Stop reading now and come back to it when you are finished.

How did you feel writing them? Read them again now. How did that feel? It is easy to assume that one would fill you with dread or revulsion, while the other would make you feel good about yourself. Perhaps that was the case.

But other reactions are possible too, like:

The negative scenario feeling 'inevitable' or a sense of "I deserve" this outcome. While the positive scenario may have seemed like 'fantasy land' or too hard to achieve.

If those reactions, or similar ones occurred, you are not alone or strange. They are a manifestation of years of conditioning from yourself and society at large. Remember, love the alcohol, and hate the alcoholic.

Facing that this message exists within your mind is vital in overcoming it. So, don't run from your feelings, 'sit' in them for a few minutes. Let them come over you, so you can really begin to let them go. Take some time to really ponder those feelings before you continue reading.

Now that you have done that, let me ask you a question. Did you mean to develop ARD, was it on purpose? Did you go inside your brain and deliberately sabotage your neurochemistry? Because that is what you would have had to do in order to deliberately develop ARD.

Did the immediate argument "Yeah, but I drank voluntarily, no one forced it down my throat!" come to mind?

Your right, no one made you drink alcohol. No one makes anyone drink alcohol (under normal circumstances).

But again, if drinking causes ARD, how is it that most people who drink never develop it? Remember, only 1:10 drinkers develop ARD. And virtually all adult people drink alcohol, many on a regular basis and still don't develop ARD. Do they?

Does the argument come into your head, yeah but they don't drink as much as I do?

Again, your right, they don't. But the real question is …why? Because, they don't like drinking alcohol? Ask any normal social drinker if they dislike the effect of alcohol and what do you think they would say?

On the other hand, ask many ARD victims if they like alcohol and a surprising number will say they don't, it feels like the devil to them. While others will describe it in terms of an obsessional type of love relationship. Still others will describe both reactions at once.

Normal drinkers never offer any descriptions like these in my experience. And I have had the opportunity to ask thousands of them. For years I did evaluations for DWI offenders who were required to submit to such evaluations as a condition of their probation. Using a few simple questions, I could easily discern the ones who had ARD from those that didn't.

Here is one such question that I found to be a reliable indicator of ARD for those that had it from birth. See how you do with it.

"Tell me about the very first time you ever had anything to drink?"

Could you answer that with a fair amount of detail? Could you describe who you were with, what the beverage was, how you felt just before you drank it, how much you drank altogether and how intoxicated you became on a 1-10 scale? Most ARD victims, especially with a family history of ARD, can answer of all those questions.

The answer from most non-ARD afflicted drinkers? "Oh, I don't know…let's see, was it when I was went fishing with my uncle and he gave me a sip of his beer to try? Hmmm or maybe…ya know, I'm just not sure, that was such a long time ago."

The difference? Brain reaction. To the person with ARD it was like the first passionate kiss in terms of importance. To the normal drinkers, more like a friendly hug as a child from a visiting grandparent, deplaning at the airport. How many people remember the former and how many the latter?

So, again I put to you, if drinking alcohol causes ARD why doesn't virtually the entire adult population have ARD?

The answer of course is that 9:10 drinkers don't have ARD because they have a normal brain reaction to alcohol. A brain reaction is very different from a mind reaction. The mind is at least partly under our volitional control. But the brain is an organ with complex and automatic reactions that are not NORMALLY under our control. ReNova will teach you how to gain control and regulate/compensate for these reactions and give you supportive tools to make that possible in the beginning. As you proceed over time the conditioned response, I have described, will help you maintain that control long term.

A part of ReNova, as mentioned before, you will have to fix the anger that can stand in the way, subconsciously, from feeling you can achieve or 'deserve' that control. So, you will come to 'forgive' yourself for having a condition that you involuntarily acquired.

ReNova will help you stay with a committed management mind set. So, follow the directions, do it all, and be well because you do deserve to be well, you and your loved ones have already suffered enough...don't you think?

Hold on to those written scenarios too, because we will make good use of them again soon.

*The Sinclair Method calls itself a cure for alcoholism, a claim that is immediately undone by the advice it gives to take a brain numbing amount of Naltrexone for the rest of your life.

Chapter 10

The Journey to Normal

The Worst Drunk

"I'm just the worst drunk", 'Ricky' said at our first meeting. Tall, Hollywood handsome, appearing to be outgoing and in his-mid-30s, he was the owner of a highly successful small business. Married with 2 small children he went on to say "I've been in all kinds of rehabs over the years, but nothing has worked. I've got to get a grip on this, I feel like my organs are dying inside me. I don't want my wife and kids to go through this anymore either. I black out every time I drink, God knows what I really do then, but I know my wife gets angry as hell and sometimes won't talk to me for days on end. I've tried NOT drinking, that doesn't work, so I'm hoping this will be different. I don't drink every day, usually 4 days a week."

When told that during his training he would have to drink every day for the process to work, he almost didn't go through with the training. But he was desperate, "so I'll try this crazy s-it… sir"

His initial laboratory ETG test verified his self-assessment and why he felt his organs were dying. His Ethyl Glucuronide level was 498,000. A number far higher than anything I had ever seen before. That number was higher than should be humanly possible… and be alive.

One other thing became clear quickly in his recovery process. In addition to being good at business and too good at drinking, he excelled in self-criticism. Also his anxiety was profoundly high. So was his restlessness. He found it hard to sit still. His leg would twitch and he was constantly shifting positions in his chair.

When the CES neuro-stimulator was applied the effect was almost immediately noticeable. The twitching stopped, he sat still for more than 2 minutes at a time and he looked much calmer.

He began on low dose Naltrexone and the neuro supplements and experienced some mild nausea that he found tolerable. It faded within a week.

He drank to blackout every night for the 1st week, combining beer openly consumed with vodka concealed in a freezer in his garage that he would sneak out and "guzzle on, whenever I can. Probably 8-10 trips but I'm not real sure"

In his 2nd week he had 3 days in which he drank to black out and 4 in which he "drank till my stupid a-s was almost blind drunk."

Week 3 he drank for him (at that point) a moderate level. A six pack of beer and usually 3 'big guzzles' off the concealed vodka each day.

By his 10th week, however, he and his wife went to the Caribbean with another couple. "I drank 5 beers over 2 days, I couldn't believe it. I really didn't want any more, I was really enjoying myself without being drunk! That hasn't happened since the 1st time I had a drink."

The weekend before his completion he went on another brief trip, hunting with his father, again drinking only a little, this time whiskey. "My dad told me I was sure was a lot more pleasant to be around now…and I am. I know it, thank God."

One more example: also close to the end of his training. He went on a Friday to a bar for 'lunch' with some friends. It was a ritual he had done dozens of times. Each time before ReNova it had been the beginning of his weekend drinking 'binge' and he would arrive home already in a black out. Not this time. An hour and a half after arriving he reported that he astonished his friends by standing up and saying "OK guys, it's been fun, gonna go back now and clear up some stuff at the office before I head home." He went on to remark "I didn't even think about how crazy that was until I was catching an Uber 3 hours later to pick up my car from the bar. Mike, what the hell have you done with Ricky… where is he?" His laughter was very real as he said that. So was his relief.

His change in personality matched the change in his drinking. When we 1st progressed beyond his initial Relaxation Response training sessions and into his mental rehearsal for self-regulation he had a response I anticipated. He felt rage at his 'Pleasure Self'. His loathing for this aspect of his personality was so bad he barely tolerated being in its 'presence' with in his mind. By the time we finished 'they' were genuine friends.

In the beginning his steady stream of self-criticism in our discussions that was incredibly intense about everything he did in his life. His 'normal' sober-self seemed to be the personification of what is described in Transactional Analysis as 'the Critical Parent'. Honestly, it was heartbreaking to watch. At one point I found myself losing objectivity, varying between wanting to hug him into silence and somehow ease his pain or slug him into silence for daring to speak so ill of a man who obviously didn't deserve the blistering critique.

But that too slowly began to change about him. By his 8th week he went almost through almost an entire discussion without a single self-criticism. By week 12 he actually said positive things about how he handled certain situations including an employee who had quit without notice.

During his follow up monthly sessions his smile was genuine and even reports of situations that were less than ideal in his life failed to illicit the blistering comments that had been his prior stock in trade.

And that vodka bottles he had hidden in the freezer? That changed to making mixed drinks and having one or two in the evening a few days a week.

How could ReNova help a man change so thoroughly in just 12 weeks? Help him go from black out drinker, killing himself with massive amounts of alcohol, to truly moderate drinker? From a man so filled with self-loathing that his every action was fodder for constant self-criticism to being able to see the good in what he does? And if it can help him change so thoroughly, can it help you as well?

The answer to these questions are better experienced than explained. So if you have all the tools, , then it is time to begin the 1st step on your journey to normal.

1-2 hours before you drink:

Our doctor advises: take your 12.5 mg. of Naltrexone* and 75mg. of Bupropion (if Bupropion keeps you awake you can take it earlier in the day)

Take your supplements*

Begin your CES device for an hour

It is best to do your relaxation response/mind training while using the CES device. It will help you achieve relaxation response more quickly and easily, speeding your results.

Even if you do not normally drink every day, do so during the initial 12 weeks. It is vital to the development of the conditioned response that will help you regulate your drinking from now on.

Plan ahead; make sure you and others are safe. Don't drink and drive or do anything that requires coordination or concentration for safety reasons.

Your drinking will gradually decrease naturally on its own. Do NOT try to force yourself to stop drinking based on will power. It will slow and/or prevent the development of the automatic and genuine 'stop' signal, that elusive thing that normal drinkers have built into their system.

How to tell the difference? It is easier than you might imagine.

Willpower is based in mastering a desire, overcoming it. In this case, mastering the desire to continue drinking. The struggle may feel mild or intense and likely can vary from day to day, drinking episode to drinking episode.

The stop signal IS A DESIRE. The desire to cease drinking because you feel satisfied and to go on drinking feels undesirable. That is how normal people stop when they do. And that is the difference between them and ARD victims.

That is what ReNova will help develop within you. You will become a normal drinker.

*When taking Naltrexone/Bupropion and supplements if you feel nausea: eat a light snack of a carb-based food.

Like a muffin, a banana etc. to overcome the nausea. NO PROTEIN. Protein will diminish the effect of your supplements.

If you find that you still feel nauseous try taking the supplements 30 minutes before taking the Naltrexone and take them both with a light snack. Soon, in as little as a week depending on your system, you will be able to skip the food and feel no nausea.

Chapter 11

Your Road Map Forward

When taking a road trip to a far-away destination it is a rare person who just jumps in the car, turns on the engine and pulls away with-out packing clothes, checking their bank balance or credit balance and getting an idea of their route. Even with today's modern GPS guidance most will want to check out lodging and sights along the way to make the journey better. Ask SIRI?

For this internal journey the same is true. Knowing what to expect and when can help keep you focused and moving ahead. It can also help family and friends who may not yet be comfortable with the idea and would prefer you quit altogether. Perhaps you also have such thoughts. They are only natural given that ARD has caused you some problems, perhaps a great many.

So, as we start, here is a reminder why to try this method 1st. Up to 80% of people fail to stay sober even 1 year after entering a traditional rehab and then going to AA. There are many 'reasons' for this, but in my opinion, based on 30 years' experience as an addiction professional they boil down to this:

Drinking does not cause ARD. ARD can exist before alcohol and it will exist until the day you draw your last breath. The latter is true whether your brain had ARD when you were born, or developed it as a reaction to alcohol after you began drinking.

ARD is caused by brain chemistry and brain function not working as they should. Take away the alcohol and the brain chemistry and brain function are still not operating as they should. Without assistance they will never function as if they are normal. That is why people who relapse to alcohol after years of sobriety quickly find themselves re-experiencing problems, because the problems were always there, lurking in the background. AA itself warns of this in their daily meetings used to help its members resist temptation.

ReNova helps you re-train your brain to function as if it is normal and show you how to keep it functioning as if it is normal. In turn you will feel and act in a normal manner, including with your drinking.

So now, let's look ahead to what you can usually expect.

WHAT TO EXPECT

ReNova Recovery Method is a process, not an event. While progress varies for everyone, you can generally expect the following based on what we see in clients at ReNova Recovery Institute:

<u>Week One</u>: After you've begun the process, taking the medications and the supplement, using the CES ultra or alpha stim device and had initial exposure to the relaxation response/visualization process very little will feel different. Your drinking is likely to continue at your previous level. However, you may feel a growing sense of desire to curtail your drinking while you're consuming alcohol. Many people attribute this to a placebo or anticipation response to beginning the treatment, but it is a direct result of beginning the use of ReNova supports.

<u>Week Two</u>: During the second week you may find that your drinking is reduced on several days although perhaps not all days for the week. Generally, this is not to goal level, but is seen as a definite improvement. You may also find that your sleep improved somewhat and that you're feeling less anxious or depressed and less

restless. These feelings will not have entirely disappeared, but will show some improvement in most cases. You may begin to have very vivid dreams and those dreams may seem quite strange, this is normal, although in no cases reported to date have these dreams had a nightmare type quality.

Week Three: Generally, about halfway through week three, drinking can reduce quite dramatically. The feelings of anxiety, depression and restlessness and problems with insomnia also show greater improvement. There may still be some days in which your drinking is more than what you'd like, but generally even these days will show improvement over previous drinking.

Week Four: It's during this week most people find that their drinking is reduced on all or most days and sometimes achieves goal level. By now a marked improvement in anxiety, depression and insomnia occur. Other people close to you may begin to comment about the changes in your drinking and the changes in your apparent mood. Your dreams may continue to become more vivid but will often feel less strange at this point.

Week Five: Week five often sees several days of regression to higher levels of drinking. This is usually not to previous levels but is higher than the week before. However, many people find that their anxiety about their drinking decreases, even though they feel concern and disappointment. The increase in drinking seen during this week is believed to be a possible response to increased brain activity due to the combination of things you are doing. It is temporary.

Week Six: During week six drinking returns to previous lows on most days although not all for most clients. Once again, especially when looking back on it with some perspective, clients tend to report that their anxiety, depression and/or insomnia continue to show some improvement. A sense of mild euphoria or calmness tends to become the dominant emotion.

Week Seven: During week seven most days are back to a lower level of drinking although one or two days may still be exceeding goal _slightly_. Euphoric or calm feeling continues, but slightly decreases and normal moods appropriate to the situations begin to occur. A sense of feeling normal begins take root.

Week Eight: During week eight most clients drink at or beneath goal without any effort or thought on their part. The sense of normalcy and balanced responses to events usually becomes quite dominant. Clients are pleasantly surprised at many of their own emotional and behavioral responses to events of their lives.

Week Nine: Week nine is also a time in which many clients find their drinking escalates backup, although again, not to previous levels before ReNova began. However, the response to this is usually neither disappointment nor concern, but rather a sense of curiosity as to why it happened. This emotionally balanced response is a part of what was seen from the previous weeks that's been building within the client. Again, we attribute this to a temporary adjustment in the brain's response to increased activity brought on by healing.

Week Ten: Now drinking returns to goal or less in most cases consistently. Most often, clients even failed to notice unless questioned about their drinking. Upon realizing that the drinking was at goal or less, the response internally tends to be more of a feeling of acceptance rather than relief. This is because feeling more normal, their drinking is now in full perspective. It has ceased to be a preoccupation or obsession and has assumed a normal secondary role in life.

Week Eleven: Commonly, clients begin to feel a sense of restlessness about completing their initial ReNova training. One of the most frequently heard comments is "I can't wait for my training to be over, so that I don't have to drink every day!" Multiple clients have either laughed or cried (a few have done both) when they realize they made that kind of statement. That's because they recognize a complete transformation in their attitude about alcohol has now occurred.

Week Twelve: Now a sense of anxiety about terminating training tends to set in. This is a reaction to losing what they perceive to be there reason for the profound change.

However, the changes occurred primarily because the client has not just acquired skills they been given, but, they've used them along with the medication, supplement and CES ultra/alpha stim device. When reminded of this most clients acknowledge it and realize that they are fully capable of continuing on their own with sufficient follow-up that could handle any problems that arise.

<u>Beyond</u>: Usually during follow-up monthly sessions clients here at ReNova Recovery Institute report a consistent pattern of adhering to the drinking limits without any real thought on their part. Within a couple of months many report an even further decrease in drinking level and frequency. The exceptions are clients who 'test the waters' by reducing the visualization exercises or discontinuing the medication or stopping the use of the supplement or too quickly reduce the use of the CES ultra/alpha stim device. In virtually all cases, when this has occurred, clients quickly recognize the error they made and return to whatever part of the routine they left off and stabilize on their own. Follow-up visits are essential however in all cases because of the <u>reinforcement exercises</u> and should be adhered to according to their schedule for the full year if this work is done with a counselor. These sessions also provide a time to share and learn from the continued adjustments in life.

Those adjustments will continue for some time. Here is an example. A client was recently in for his follow up. He reported that he realized that even though it had been 7 months since his drinking had been out of control he still found himself "skulking towards the refrigerator and opening the beer as quietly as possible, just like I did when I was trying to keep my wife from figuring out I was having another one. But here I am still acting like I'm doing something 'bad.' It really hit me how messed up that is, so I've come up with an affirmation "Even though I have alcoholism I don't behaving like an alcoholic".

If you are doing this on your own, I strongly suggest you share your thoughts with someone close to you. You will find this much easier to do now because the level of threat sensitivity, prompted by your Amygdala will be greatly reduced. That 'walled off' sense will be gone. You and others will notice this in virtually all cases.

One other thing will be reduced too, your tolerance for alcohol. By the time you finish your initial training, 2 drinks will usually produce the same reaction in you as they do in people who don't have ARD, relative to your same age, sex and weight. In other words… you will be a cheap date!

Chapter 12

Starting Recovery

<u>Your 1st Day</u>

Always do these exercises before you drink any alcohol!

Initial self-exercise :

Close your eyes.

Start with 3 deep breaths in through the nose, out through the mouth.

Then count backwards from 50-1 slowly. **<u>Between each number think "relax".</u>**

When you get to the number 1 tell yourself, "every time I practice, I can get more relaxed with less effort."

Then tell yourself: "I'm getting better and better" "Negative thoughts no longer affect me" and "Every day I'm more motivated for alcohol moderation".

Recall the two possible outcomes you wrote about (re-reading them before hand is a good idea).

Then tell yourself: "I'm going to count from 1-5 and open my eyes feeling awake and refreshed." Then count 1-5 slowly and open your eyes. Remind yourself as soon as you open your eyes "I feel awake and refreshed."

So, what have you accomplished? A great deal, although it is unlikely (yet) to feel like much. Your compulsion to over drink is almost certain to feel unchanged. Remember, Do not try to force yourself to stop or moderate your drinking. Willpower doesn't work. ReNova does work.

Days 2-10

Days 2-10 are an exact repeat of day one, except you reduce the starting number by 5 each day 45-40-35-30 etc. until you are starting at the number 10.

After the tenth day you will begin to do some vital work designed to give you long term control of alcohol and relief from the true cause of 'alcoholism' your brain's reactions.

Change Is Good

"Sure man, why not? I've been looking for a way to handle this for a while. What have I got to lose?"

John, a bank officer at a nationally prominent 'investor's' bank seemed to have a truly open mind. Something of a 'man for all seasons' he was equally at home stepping in to the ring for a mixed martial arts bout (which he had done throughout his twenties) or attending the symphony to which he purchased season tickets each year.

Highly organized and detail oriented he agonized over the smallest details. His affect: polished- professional-macho, hid deep anxiety and low self-esteem. The anxiety came through daily to co-workers who often remarked on his 'high strung' moments. It also showed in his blood pressure, which was high for a man who ate well and was in top physical shape. His blood pressure, he said, had been high "well before drinking got the better of me."

A regular church goer, he felt deep shame about his drinking which had gotten steadily worse over the decade prior to his entering ReNova. He had made many attempts to control it on his own, without success.

When he was out with friends or coworkers, he would have 1 or 2 beers, then race to the store on the way home and pick up a supply to drink alone in secret.

Secrecy had gotten a lot easier to maintain just prior to trying ReNova because his wife had divorced him. Childless, he had no one at home to watch him deteriorate into drunken depression. A friend and neighbor, familiar with ReNova, was watching though, with growing concern. Waiting until the time was right, he offered him this solution.

"Sure man, why not… what have I got to lose?"

John visited his doctor, who knew about his drinking and got a prescription of Naltrexone and a pill cutter at my suggestion. He began on the ¼ standard dose of 12.5 mg. of the medication.

One week later, he started on the supplements we formulated at ReNova Institute. He began using an Alpha-stim the same day. He used it daily for one hour as suggested.

At his first session of Relaxation Response training he achieved the state well and was able to envision the desired outcome. "That felt great. We'll see if it works man, thanks."

Like many clients he was skeptical not just of the process but also the idea of drinking every day. "I usually take a day or two off a week, it seems to help me"

"Has it really helped you?" I remarked. "Hasn't your drinking gotten more and more out-of-control despite the 'days off'? If you were training for a fight, would you take some days off to help you rest up for it?" "No man, I wouldn't, ok drink daily, got it" he said, still sounding reluctant. "Good" I said, "because this is a fight and it's one you can win."

And he did win.

<u>John, one year later</u>:

"I'm at a point of genuine satisfaction with my life, I have never been happier."

It had been quite a year. John kept a daily diary of his drinking for the 1st several months. It showed a pattern almost identical to the average 'What to Expect' noted above.

The change in reactions went well beyond alcohol. People at work began to ask him what he was doing to 'keep it together' so well. "The joke is, now I'm the one keeping everyone else calm when things get hairy."

Work wasn't the only place he showed a different attitude. One day, about 2 months after entering ReNova, John came home to find that his upstairs bathroom had developed a leak. His brand-new kitchen cabinets immediately below were ruined. "Man, before this I would have lost it. It would have ruined my whole week, if not my whole month. But all I thought was, ok go turn off the water and call the contractor again. I was upset of course but it didn't feel like the end of the world."

His ability to be open about his thoughts and express his wants without conflicted feelings increased. "I went on a trip to Vegas with some guy friends and they all wanted to save money by sharing a big hotel suite. I just told them 'no' if they can't afford their own rooms then sorry, but I can and I am getting one for myself. I couldn't have done that before. I would have just gone along with it and been miserable putting up with them in my space. Now, I didn't feel the least bit bad turning down their suggestion. I also thought I lost my credit card while I was there and I didn't get upset, just retraced my steps until I found it. Wanna know how much I drank Mike? I dunno, I didn't keep track, I've stopped doing that cause it just not important anymore, I trust myself now. I can tell you this though, I didn't get drunk, never drank beyond a little buzz feeling…in Vegas! I came home with more money than I left with too."

His blood pressure? "Never gets over 120/80."

His drinking? "Under excellent control."

His ex-wife? "Dating me again."

Their previously poor sex life? "She can't keep her hands off me now."

John was so convinced of his change and the power of ReNova that he went to the national CEO of his bank and told him what he had done, suggesting ReNova to him as an investment opportunity. John is the investment risk analyst at the branch of bank where he is employed.

Days 11-30

Now we move beyond commitment reinforcement to resolving the internal conflict that may keep you from solving your brain reaction problem.

This deserves some explaining before we get to the use of the technique. We will be using a process loosely based on a type of therapy known as Gestalt.

What exactly is Gestalt Psychotherapy? Developed by a German neo Freudian named Fritz Perls, Gestalt is a process of imagining yourself dividing the parts of your psychological sum. Having achieved that imaginary division, you would start a dialogue between the different parts of yourself. The goal is to explore the needs of these different 'you(s)' and then negotiate ways to meet those needs in a beneficial way that prevents self-defeating behaviors and solves internal conflicts.

In classic Gestalt Therapy a counselor would ask you to focus 1st on some aspect of awareness that is physical, such as your breathing and proceed to broaden your awareness of your physicality and environment in a step by step fashion causing you to gradually become 'hyper alert' to yourself and the sensations you are aware of experiencing. This would continue through to your mind until finally you become aware of the different 'selves' with in you.

Then, in classic Gestalt you would imagine these different selves placed nearby (such as a chair across the room, a corner, a couch etc.) Serving as the 'executive' self you would then be asked to dialogue out loud with these different selves as the counselor guides you to 'probe' for needs underlying certain behaviors or blocks to success and to find ways to resolve them. Typically, this process results in divisions into more selves as you keep exploring different aspects of your life and behaviors.

There are two problems with using classic Gestalt with ARD victims:

First in ARD a mild kind of hyper alertness or hyper vigilance tends to be present at all times. This can cause psychological discomfort by the increasing alertness used in the Gestalt technique. That is because of the association between alertness and its root cause in ARD; an over active Amygdala that prompts feelings of anxiety. The more alert an ARD victim becomes, the more anxious they may become as well.

Secondly as any mental health professional will tell that has dealt with an ARD victim, ARD results in over thinking everything. The term analysis paralysis may not have been coined specifically about ARD victims but it strongly applies!

The above being true classic Gestalt was not used with great success with ARD victims. The theory underlying the technique however is of tremendous value to ARD victims because of the split off of personality that is so common with ARD.

Chapter 13

"Dr. Jekyll, May I Introduce Mr. Hyde"

"Turning…turning…revolution complete." A line from a classic play/movie in which an alcoholic named Michael is being commented on by a friend. The friend has many times watched Michael get intoxicated and go from friendly and caring to nasty and psychologically abusive to everyone around him. Sobering up somewhat later in the presentation Michael then heads to a late night mass in an attempt to assuage his feelings of guilt for having over drank- only vaguely remembering his actions. The clear implication is that it is a solution he has tried many times…with no success. Still he seems to have a desperate desire for somehow, someway to make it work. 'Maybe this time…no…but let me try anyway' the all too obvious look on his face as he grabs his coat to head out the door, the cycle never ending.

For some the experience noted above will have a hard ring of truth it. For others the transformation can be the exact opposite. Or it can be going from quiet and shy, to loud and boisterous or vice a versa.

"En vino veritas."In wine there is truth." *Or is there?* Alcohol loosens restrictions, governors on judgment and behaviors. What results, however, is a *distorted* expression of behaviors that are normally suppressed. These behaviors can, and sometimes are, expressed when fully sober. It is closer to say "In wine is caricature" Is a caricature the truth?

Think for a moment about any caricature drawing you may have seen. The features are greatly distorted for exaggeration. If the drawing is of a famous person or someone you know well, you can undoubtedly see the resemblance. But, is that the way you would describe them to a police sketch artist if no picture was available and they were missing?

And if you were assigned to search for someone you didn't know, or recognize due to celebrity, in a large and crowded area, how easily would you spot them based on that kind of sketch?

 As this caricature keeps showing up in an intoxicated state ARD victims, their family and friends come to accept it as truth. It is a 'truth' most ARD victims cordially loathe about themselves. Yet the relentless drive within the brain's deeper recesses keeps calling for the very substance that causes this caricature to emerge: to taunt, disgust, shock and even harm.

By the time many ARD victims start to address their problem, this image is deeply held in their psyche. ARD victims tend to confuse the caricature for their true pleasure-seeking side that all humans possess. Because of this they tend in early recovery to deprive themselves of all types of normal pleasure (unless they too have an addictive quality such as gambling, over eating etc.). Of course, this state cannot hold forever. Either they learn to adjust to having normal fun or they go deeper into addictive pursuits as a substitute for alcohol, or they relapse back to alcohol itself.

Eventually many seek 'serenity' and spirituality in an obsessive manner as a substitute for alcohol and other addictions. I have known several friends and family members to attend 3 or 4 different kinds of 12 step programs at a time in a sadly desperate attempt to wall themselves off from life in a cocoon of groups, sponsors and constant reading of various books on how to 'surrender'.

Many rehabs do include structured leisure in an attempt to overcome this problem, but they fail to address the real cause of why it is a needed part of treatment. As a result, the learning tends not to 'stick' with the client once they 'graduate' in 28 days and go home.

ReNova will now help you address this head on in a healthy manner. To do so we will take the process and divide it into 3 separate stages:

Control

Reconciliation

Integration

Control is what we will achieve in days 11-30.

To start, remember to follow all steps for what to do each day of your initial training. You will not however need your two alternate life scripts. By now they should be clearly imprinted on your psyche in a way that is strong enough that the ReNova reinforcement technique should be enough.

How to Proceed

Read the 'script' below. Remember to do your best to memorize it. A reminder: memorization is greatly helped by visually imagining the described scenario as you read it. This puts the information more firmly into the brain. Read it several times using this technique and then close your eyes and recreate it entirely as if you are watching a movie. Once done open your eyes and re-read taking note of anything you may have forgotten. Then repeat the process until you have a complete memory of it. Typically this will take about 1-2 hours depending on the strength of your memory, so make sure you have the time to devote to it when you begin. If you are working with a counselor or using the audio recordings we make available that will help speed up the process and make it easier because you will have already experienced the exercise, but include the reading anyway. Remember: in it to win it.

Use your count down exercise. Go to your ideal place of relaxation. Mentally repeat the following statements to yourself:

Every day I'm getting better and better

Negative thoughts and suggestions no longer influence me

Every day I become more motivated for alcohol moderation.

Invite your alter ego into your ideal place of relaxation. This is your pleasure self. This is the side of you that uses alcohol as a means to relax and feel good. Think about how you feel about this part of yourself, and how it has treated you, be honest about it. Look at this aspect of yourself and realize something. No matter what you do, no matter where you go, your pleasure self is always going to be with you because it a natural and inseparable part of you. So you have a choice; be at emotional war with this part of yourself or develop a better understanding and relationship with it.

Now switch perspectives. Imagine you are your pleasure self, looking at your responsibility self. This is the side of you that wants to 'be good', take care of things and succeed in life. Think about how you feel about this part of yourself, and how it has treated you, be honest about it. Look at this aspect of yourself and realize something. No matter what you do, no matter where you go, your responsibility self is always going to be with you because it a natural and in separable part of you. So you have a choice; be at emotional war with this part of yourself or develop a better understanding and relationship with it.

Now switch your mind back to your responsibility self and let the two different selves approach each other. When just a few feet apart, stop and look at pleasure you and mentally say "ok, truce, we need to start over." Your pleasure side says,"ok truce, let's start over."

Your pleasure side walks away.

Now find a movie theater seat in your ideal place, with a movie screen a short distance away. Sit down in the seat and begin to see a movie in your mind.

On the screen you see your pleasure side in his/her most common drinking setting. Watch as he/she drinks to what is a normal limit (2-3-4 drinks perhaps) then freeze the movie.

Once it is frozen get up from the seat and join your pleasure side on the screen. Walk up to your 'frozen self' and let them know you are there. Say to them that you are ok with them having a good time, but you want to avoid any problems. Ask him/her to stop drinking now.

Sense that your pleasure side is going to cooperate, then un-freeze the movie. Spend the rest of the entire day/night with your pleasure side all the way through to bedtime seeing them not taking any more drinks but feeling good and content.

Now imagine you are in your bedroom but it now has two beds. See your pleasure side getting in one of them. Look at your pleasure side and tell him/her you are proud of them, they did a good job. Sense that your pleasure side is proud of him/her self. _Tell your pleasure self to have a dream and in the dream they are feeling proud of them self and they are enjoying the process_.

Then get in your bed and _fall asleep having the same dream_.

In the morning you wake up and go back to the movie theater seat. There is your pleasure self, sleeping in the movie.

Now move the screen slightly upward and see yourself 5 years in the future. Perceive that this future you is looking back over the last 5 years. He/she is thinking about what a good job they have done being in control of drinking. Your future self is considering why that is and realizes that it is because they did this exercise every single day and took their medication as long as needed, took their supplements as long as they needed, used their CES as long as they needed and still use it occasionally to give their brain a healthy boost.

But more than that has happened. All of your best qualities, those things you like about yourself have gotten stronger and better, while the qualities you don't like about yourself and gotten less and less. Perceive your 5 year future self thinking about what these specific good and less desirable qualities are that have changed.

Now see a beautiful bluish/white light come down and surround the screen, then surround you as well. Perceive love, peace, power, acceptance and protection from this light.

Let the light pull away taking the screen with it as it moves quickly off into infinity. Perceive you still feel the love, peace, power, acceptance and protection.

Now count the numbers 1-5 to yourself mentally and open your eyes.

As you do this exercise daily, concentrate on feeling a little less angry and a little more accepting each day between your two sides until you feel more neutral and accepting of each aspect of yourself.

Although rare you may already feel that way. If that is the case, then just focus on the next suggestion only:

Each day work to become more aware and accepting of the fact that no matter what, both sides you exist, will always exist, and need each other for a healthy life to be possible.

How did you feel doing this exercise the 1st time? Anger at yourself, even revulsion perhaps? That is the most common way clients have described their emotions when 'confronting' their pleasure side. Now you know why when people 'try' using simpler methods like just medication or AA they usually fail. Because after all, why would you do something important on a daily basis to help out someone you can barely stand to be around?

How People Choose a Counselor

Take a moment to consider and rate the following characteristics of an addiction counselor. Decide which would cause you to choose one over another. Imagine that you have had a consultation with a few and are 'sizing them up.' Rate each characteristic on a 1 to 10 scale.

Has personal or similar life experiences to mine____

Seemed to genuinely care about me and my recovery____

Has warmth and a sense of humor____

Appears non-judgmental____

Complimented me on the courage I had to seek help____

Appears knowledgeable about addiction____

Has a PHD in psychology ____

Office is conveniently located to home or work____

Has convenient hours____

Was aloof and detached____

'Confronted' me on being two minutes late to session____

Told me that they expect payment at start of session____

Looked at the clock several times during session____

Told me I was "probably in denial" about how bad off I was____

Asked more questions about how spouse and children were handling things than about me____

If you are like most people the 1st 6 characteristics were rated highly on the scale. The middle 3 were rated in a mid-ranking. The last 6 were ranked low on the scale.

Did you find it odd that ranking a counselor to work with would appear in this place in the book? Well it was and it wasn't. That's because whether you work with a counselor on this or not, the most important counselor you have is *you*.

Think back to the exercise and your pleasure self for a moment. Think about how the two sides of you felt about 'the other'. How is your pleasure self ever going to cooperate with someone who is judgmental, perhaps even emotionally abusive and wants little more than for he/she to go away?

So again, over the next 20 days concentrate in your exercise on imagining feeling less and less negatively about your pleasure self and instead begin thinking about how the two of you have a chance to 'get right' with one another. DON'T MISS A SINGLE DAY OF DOING THIS EXERCISE. If you do it will be necessary to start over from day one in order for this to work. Remember: In it to win it.

Chapter 14

Befriending Your Other Self

Acting To Believe

"I can't believe this is working. I mean… I hoped it would and it made sense the way you explained it. But I'm really drinking a lot less and the other stuff I'm seeing in my 5-year self is already happening." 'Roger' a stage and animation voice actor said as he laughed in a slightly embarrassed way. Roger had been referred by a therapist of a family member to get help for his drinking problem. Originally, he had intended to try for full sobriety, but when the options were explained to him, he chose moderation instead…as do most client at ReNova.

About 4 weeks into his therapy he began seeing a significant drop in his drinking and so did his fiancé. He was very much in love and very concerned about losing his relationship and that had prompted his seeking help. Like many younger ARD victims he initially thought his heavy drinking was "just a phase" that would pass as he progressed into his mid-20's as it did for many of his friends. Instead the opposite happened. The more he tried to control it using will power the worse it seemed to get.

His self-confidence and self-esteem were taking a serious hit as a result. His sex drive was already starting to lower as a result of both over drinking and guilt for over drinking. He wasn't trying as hard as he once did for roles and he was confused and slightly depressed.

As we began to move into the reconciliation phase of his training, he became unsure again. Could he really make friends with his drinking self? He had succeeded in developing a state of 'truce' and that felt to him like a major accomplishment that coincided with his increased drinking control. But learn to like that part of himself? That seemed like a stretch to him. Being an actor, I instructed him to play it as a role. He was to act like he liked the other half of him and to really immerse himself into the 'part'. Taking it from that perspective he could psychologically embrace the process.

Soon he and his other 'half' were engaged in happy conversation 'talking' about girls, roles he played, friends, upcoming events and more. It didn't take long before the feelings of friendship with the other part of himself were genuine. His sex drive went back up "I've become a tiger and my girlfriend loves it." He took on a side job selling and eventually reconciled with the fact that as much as Dallas felt like home, success was New York or Los Angeles for his dreams.

'Roger' One Year Later:

"Hello Mike, I can't believe it has been a year already. Well, the drinking is splendid. I usually drink just two maybe three drinks and only a couple of times per week. Last night was St. Patrick's Day. I had 4 beers which is the most I have had in one sitting in several weeks. My wife and I moved to New York to pursue our theater careers. I've continued to practice the daily relaxing meditation. I've also gotten into green tea, running and breathing exercises. I use the Alpha-Stim for at least an hour every week. The anxiety is a lot better, sometimes comes back, but not as severe and I can control it. Sobriety is a great thing"

Note that last statement-Sobriety is a great thing. He no longer feels like his level of drinking even rises to a significance that it matters, he is living a 'sober' lifestyle in his mind and so it is.

Do the following exercise for the next 30 days.

Use your 10-1 countdown. Go to your ideal place of relaxation. Mentally repeat the following statements to yourself:

Everyday I'm getting better and better

Negative thoughts and suggestions no longer influence me

Everyday I become more motivated for alcohol moderation and the benefits that brings

Invite your alter ego into your ideal place of relaxation. Now the two of you are feeling much better about one another. Concentrate on the good aspects of your pleasure side. What has it brought to you over the years from childhood on? What do you like about this side of yourself? Now switch perspectives, concentrate on what your responsibility side has done for your pleasure side from childhood on? What does your pleasure side like about the responsibility side of you? Imagine that the two sides of you sit down together and have a conversation like two old friends about anything that comes to mind. After a short time your pleasure side gets up and walks away smiling and you are smiling too.

Now find your movie theater seat in your ideal place, with your movie screen a short distance away. Sit down in the seat and begin to see a set of brief movies in your mind.

On the screen you see your pleasure side in his/her most common drinking setting. Watch as he/she drinks to what is a normal limit (2-3-4 drinks perhaps) then freeze the movie.

Once it is frozen get up from the seat and join your pleasure side on the screen. Walk up to your 'frozen self' and let them know you are there. Say to them that you are ok with them having a good time, but you want to avoid any problems. Ask him/her to stop drinking now.

Sense that your pleasure side is going to cooperate, then unfreeze the movie. Spend the rest of the entire day/night with your pleasure side all the way through to bedtime seeing them not taking any more drinks but feeling good and content.

Now move to a new scene. One that isn't the most common but does happen in your life. Repeat the scenario as before.

Now, change to another scene, this is a special occasion scene. A birthday, holiday, party etc. see your pleasure side drinking slightly more as people tend to on these occasions. Not out of control just a little more. Then repeat the process all the way through to bedtime, remembering to tell your pleasure side you are proud of him or her, they did a great job and reminding as in the prior two scenes to dream they are proud of themselves and enjoying the process. Make sure you imagine yourself doing the same.

Then, after the last scene see you and your pleasure side in the morning both sitting in theater seats watching the screen.

Now move the screen slightly upward and see yourself 5 years in the future. Perceive that this future you is looking back over the last 5 years. He/she is thinking about what a good job they have done being in control of drinking. Your future self is considering why that is and realizes that it is because they did this exercise every single day and took their medication as long as needed, took their supplements as long as they needed, used their CES as long as they needed and still use it occasionally to give their brain a healthy boost.

But more than that has happened. All of your best qualities, those things you like about yourself have gotten stronger and better, while the qualities you don't like about yourself and gotten less and less. Perceive your 5 year future self thinking about what these specific good and less desirable qualities are that have changed.

Now see a beautiful bluish/white light come down and surround the screen, then surround you as well. Perceive love, peace, power, acceptance and protection from this light.

Let the light pull away taking the screen with it as it moves quickly off into infinity. Perceive you still feel the love, peace, power, acceptance and protection. See your pleasure side smile at you and say good bye and then get up and walk away.

Now count the numbers 1-5 to yourself mentally and open your eyes.

Chapter 15

Informing and Shaping Your Subconscious Mind

I knew I was addicted from the very 1st time I used a drug. I was 13 years old-far too young. It was the time of the hippies, at the start of the 1970's. They would gather in what was then called Lee Park in Dallas. I took LSD. When finished I wanted more...immediately. My brother, who had a natural brain defense against addiction, tried to explain to me that I should wait a month, drink a lot of orange juice and then when I 'tripped' again it would feel just as good. My response? I grabbed him by his t-shirt and said "No, I have found it, and I don't want to come down, now can you find me some more?"

Because addiction was rife in my family I already knew about AA and I knew what my response meant. I didn't care at the time. Within months, I did care and went to an NA group (the biggest and 1st off shoot AA, Narcotics Anonymous was formed in the early 1950's)

It didn't last long. That started a cycle of lapse, get clean, lapse, and get clean. I eventually switched to AA having gone through a variety of drugs. But, the cycle stayed the same no matter what the drug.

I couldn't relate to the steps. I knew, watching many others relapse that had worked them, they had a limited potential to help. I wasn't and still am not an atheist or agnostic. I had been through 2 near death experiences, both related to cars. I know that physical life is not the end, with the same sureity that I know physical life exists.

'The steps' weren't a real answer to me because they were about a passive 'surrender' approach and I am a fighter at heart. But the group meetings helped, I thought, to at least some degree.

In May 1986 I found a book "The Power of Your Subconscious Mind" by Joseph Murphy. Less than half way through the short read I found myself thinking, "I've found it!" Those words hit me hard. The same words I had used 16 years earlier about LSD and with the same passion.

I didn't use another substance until I had a drink on my birthday in October of 2018. I knew I was safe because of ReNova and I have remained safe, a perfectly normal social drinker. Not only is my drinking not out-of-control, I feel perfectly content with or without alcohol. I never felt that way when drinking/using drugs in the old days. My use before was always obsessional and compulsive.

If I had not developed ReNova, it still would be. Former AA members abound that serve as proof of that.

A vital part Of ReNova was born with my discovery of "The Power of Your Subconscious Mind"

I have recommended the book over the years to many patients in the treatment centers in which I worked and directed.

The ability to shape how our minds think and the corresponding effect on our subconscious processes is undeniable.

For many years I advised my patients to begin each day with 3 thoughts about their good qualities before they get out of bed. I instructed them to give themselves specific examples of how they have demonstrated those qualities in their lives. Then as they drifted off to sleep to review their accomplishments for the day. ONLY their accomplishments, no failures allowed.

The result on mood, behavior and outlook was obvious in those that followed the advice. In as little as a few weeks they would begin to see themselves with a wholly different perspective.

How? It is very simple. Research has shown again and again that what we dream effects our waking emotional states and our waking emotional state effects our dreams. What we think about as we 1st wake up sets our mood for the day to a surprising degree. So, if you have and recall good qualities about yourself then you see yourself as a good person. What we think about just before we drift off to sleep is generally the 1st thing we dream about at night. What we dream about becomes implanted in our subconscious thought process. So, just using these two simple techniques daily starts a positive cycle of self-belief based on facts. We can argue with ourselves about self-worth all we want. Those arguments can be filled with many negative messages: from parents, teachers, preachers and society in general. But we cant dispute what we have done. So, thinking of ways in which we actually demonstrate our positive qualities is indisputable. Reviewing what we have actually accomplished that was positive is also indisputable. Once that habit is ingrained in the mind it is a lot harder to let negative older messages drift by unnoticed or unchallenged or to feel them with the same sting.

Now, consider this. How many times in your life have you awakened form a dream or nightmare and found yourself having an emotional response either pleasant or fearful? If you were ever sober for an extended period of time you may even have had dreams in which you were drinking again. If so you may have even awakened feeling drunk and/or confused about whether it actually happened. AA members frequently speak about 'drunk dreams', they are a very common phenomenon.

But, what happens when you dream you are enjoying something, as in you are enjoying controlling your alcohol use? What happens when you dream you are proud of yourself for doing such a good job controlling your alcohol use?

That is exactly what you are conditioning your mind to dream. Every night. It is a part of your script, for self-control. "Tell your pleasure self to dream about the fact that they are liking controlling their alcohol use and they are proud of themselves. Then get in your bed and drift off to sleep having the same dream."

Not only are you telling yourself to have those dreams, you are telling yourself that while at a deeply relaxed level of mental functioning. The brain wave that is active when we dream is called the Alpha brain wave. You are using that same brain wave in the deeply relaxed state.

There are three parts to this aspect of ReNova:

a) You are telling yourself you ARE controlling your alcohol use.

b) You like controlling your alcohol use.

c) You are proud of yourself for controlling your alcohol use.

Let's break those down:

You are controlling your alcohol use. At the same time as the medication and supplements are reducing your desire to over drink you begin to dream about the fact you are controlling alcohol. The objective fact supports the subjective thought/dream command. And just like with Pavlov's dogs you are setting up a conditioned response. But unlike Pavlov's dogs you will not stop having the response when the medication is slowly withdrawn because you are programming yourself every day to continue to have it.

Try this experiment now to understand how this relates to actual physiological response. Read this and follow this brief simple script:

Close your eyes, VIVIDLY imagine you are in a desert. You have been walking alone through this desert for several days. No water, no shelter. There is a big sandstorm blowing. You are trudging to walk against the wind. You are exhausted by the effort. The storm blows sand into your eyes, nose and mouth. Your mouth fills with the sand but you can do nothing about it. You are parched and have no saliva with which to expel it. Now open your eyes.

Does your mouth feel dry? If you imagined it vividly enough it does. Why? Because your mind cannot distinguish what you are vividly imagining and what you are actually experiencing.

This is the exact same principle that many Olympic athletes now incorporate into their training program, including the medal winning Jamaican bobsled team. They had no snow. They imagined bobsledding over and over again and doing it flawlessly...and they won. They trained their bodies to perform/respond as if they had snow to work with in actual practice.

You are not only training your mind daily by seeing yourself drinking less you are training your subconscious mind to believe it as well. Whatever we see ourselves doing and believe both consciously and subconsciously that we are doing, we do.

The more we see/imagine ourselves doing something, the more our subconscious mind is trained to believe it, the more our bodies begin doing it. Our brain is an organ, it is a part of the body, it can learn/relearn and over learn anything with sufficient exposure. Eventually it will respond by dialing down the 'go signal' neurochemicals on its own and dial up the 'stop signal' neurochemicals on its own as a response to what it perceives/believes is happening without the support of the medication/supplements.

You are liking controlling your alcohol use. Even the most motivated among us sometimes have trouble doing something we 'know' is good for us or 'needs' to be done. But,who has trouble doing something they really enjoy doing? When we procrastinate it is usually by doing something we would rather do. then something we need to do... isn't it? So, when you program your mind to enjoy controlling your alcohol use as opposed to 'needing' to control your alcohol use you get the result of actively pursuing as a sense of pleasure. Adding it to the dream sequence embeds it it into the mind in a powerful way.

You are proud of yourself for controlling your alcohol use. Adding this to the dream sequence further reinforces your motivation to continue the process. Although this might seem unneeded because it should be a natural response, remember the societal conditioning: love the alcohol...hate the alcoholic. Restoring and reinforcing self-pride at every level of the mind is essential to overcome potential self-sabotage. So, remember to add this to your dream order every night.

Chapter 16

Embracing Your Shadow

<u>Too Smart To Be Dumb</u>

"I have had it with AA and standard rehab." Ralph, an Ivy League college grad said as he sat down in the chair. Several minutes into his initial consultation he seemed slightly speechless, a state far from common for this highly intelligent and articulate man.

I had gone through a list of questions I normally ask people, but they are not what would seem like normal questions asked in an alcoholism consultation.

When you were a child did you sleep well or poorly? Did your sleep pattern change a lot when you went through puberty? Do you get sleepy within an hour or so of eating carbohydrate-based foods? Were you super ambitious feeling well into your twenties? Has it fallen off noticeably since your mid 30's? Did you have a period in your 20's when you seemed to slow down on alcohol then pick back up in your 30's? Has your drinking 'ski sloped' now that you are in your 40's? When was the last time you had your testosterone level checked? Etc.

That I predicted his responses to many of the questions before he had a chance to answer seemed even more perplexing to him than the questions themselves.

Long experience in the field, combined with a certainty that ARD is an involuntary brain reaction, has taught me to ask those questions. It has also enabled me be able to guess the answers, based on the 1st couple of answers given along with affect and physical appearance.

The questions aren't random or pointless. They provide real insight into the ways in which the problem with alcohol started and how ReNova might help solve it.

That Ralph could see the questions were genuine was a great advantage on the start of his real recovery. Ralph travels a lot in his work and while drinking at home was frequently out of control, it was the road trips where it escalated the most. Black outs that sometimes started as soon as the airport bar, could start a binge that consumed each day of the trip. Hang overs, irritability and brain fog had become everyday realities to him.

Ralph had been involved with AA for several years and like most he had quite few lapses. Standard inpatient and outpatient treatments had failed to curb the lapses and he decided to try something else.

Unlike many patients I didn't have to convince him of the possibility of successful moderation, only explain the basics of the process. His keen mind had little trouble making sense of the brain reaction disorder concept. He also grasped well the logic that fixing the real problem, the brain reaction, was the real key to ending his active ARD. Doing so leaving him free to drink like others, with control.

The biggest challenge with Ralph, like with so many, was stopping the anger and self-criticism.

Ralph's biggest advantage is that he is highly methodical and organized, although he doesn't really see himself in that way. He went about following directions well and regularly.

The payoff was almost immediate. He exceeded goal reduction faster than most. His escalation periods at week 5 and 9 were not nearly as pronounced as normal, but I had quite a time getting him to see that. "Oh how normal of you" became a regular retort to his very minor variances from goal. You sound just like a man who varies the level of his drinking according to circumstances, instead of some rigid rule, but still keeps control. Shame on you!"

Sarcastic laughter usually worked to get him to see he was actually more than OK, he was doing well.

When it came time to go beyond 'befriending' his other self and integrating the two halves of his personality the old trepidation showed up. But being methodical and the rule follower he refuses to see himself as, paid off.

Ralph Today:

"My wife has stopped counting my drinks and I have too. Now when we go out I'm the DD. We have worked through a lot of her undermining me in front of the kids. It was just a habit she developed from when I used to overreact 'cause I was hung over and irritable. Don't get hangovers any more. That's because I don't get drunk anymore when I drink. In fact, my wife usually drinks more than I do and she doesn't have a drinking problem, never has had one. I tell ya though, just not losing my cool all the time has been worth the price of admission. Not taking anything away from the less drinking of course."

Now it is time to integrate the 2 sides: Dr. Jekyll and Mr. Hyde. Because, they have always been one in the same. Real freedom come not just by liking yourself but by truly accepting yourself.

Do This Exercise for the next 30 days

Use your 10-1 countdown. Go to your ideal place of relaxation. Mentally repeat the following statements to yourself:

Everyday I'm getting better and better

Negative thoughts and suggestions no longer influence me

Everyday I become more motivated for alcohol moderation and the benefits that brings

Invite your alter ego into your ideal place of relaxation. Now the two of you are feeling much better about one another. Concentrate on the good aspects of your pleasure side. What has it brought to you over the years from childhood on? What do you like about this side of yourself? Now switch perspectives, concentrate on what your responsibility side has done for your pleasure side from childhood on? What does your pleasure side like about the responsibility side of you? Imagine that the two sides of you sit down together and have a conversation like two old friends about anything that comes to mind. After a short time your pleasure side gets up and walks away smiling and you are smiling too.

Now find your movie theater seat in your ideal place, with your movie screen a short distance away. Sit down in the seat and begin to see a set of brief movies in your mind.

On the screen you see your pleasure side in his/her most common drinking setting. Watch as he/she drinks to what is a normal limit (2-3-4 drinks perhaps) then freeze the movie.

Once it is frozen get up from the seat and join your pleasure side on the screen. Walk up to your 'frozen self' and let them know you are there. Say to them that you are ok with them having a good time, but you want to avoid any problems. Ask him/her to stop drinking now.

Sense that your pleasure side is going to cooperate, then unfreeze the movie. Spend the rest of the entire day/night with your pleasure side all the way through to bedtime seeing them not taking any more drinks but feeling good and content.

Now move to a new scene. One that isn't the most common but does happen in your life. Repeat the scenario as before.

Now, change to another scene, this is a special occasion scene. A birthday, holiday, party etc. see your pleasure side drinking slightly more as people tend to on these occasions. Not out of control just a little more. Then repeat the process all the way through to bedtime, remembering to tell your pleasure side you are proud of him or her, they did a great job and reminding as in the prior two scenes to dream they are proud of themselves and enjoying the process. Make sure you imagine yourself doing the same.

Then, after the last scene see you and your pleasure side in the morning both sitting in theater seats watching the screen.

Now move the screen slightly upward and see yourself 5 years in the future. Perceive that this future you is looking back over the last 5 years. He/she is thinking about what a good job they have done being in control of drinking. Your future self is considering why that is and realizes that it is because they did this exercise every single day and took their medication as long as needed, took their supplements as long as they needed, used their CES as long as they needed and still use it occasionally to give their brain a healthy boost.

But more than that has happened. All of your best qualities, those things you like about yourself have gotten stronger and better, while the qualities you don't like about yourself and gotten less and less. Perceive your 5 year future self thinking about what these specific good and less desirable qualities are that have changed.

Now see a beautiful bluish/white light come down and surround the screen, then surround you as well. Perceive love, peace, power, acceptance and protection from this light.

Let the light pull away taking the screen with it as it moves quickly off into infinity. Perceive you still feel the love, peace, power, acceptance and protection. *See your pleasure side smile at you and then get up and step inside you. Concentrate of feeling this part of yourself being there. Welcome the feeling.*

Now count the numbers 1-5 to yourself mentally and open your eyes.

Chapter 17

The 5 Year Integration

How many times have you driven a familiar route, found yourself lost in your thoughts and arrived not realizing how far you have driven or how long a time you were on the road? Or, became absorbed in watching a show, a game, or some other absorbing activity and the time seemed to fly by? Or perhaps gotten lost in a daydream at work and when you 'came to' realized that you are now behind?

Psychologists tell us perception of time is highly subjective and the above examples are rich proof they are right. When we are not focused on what we are doing time seems to go faster. Why? Again, the answer is the alpha brain wave, when we are absorbed or in reverie it is the more active brain wave cycle. It simply doesn't perceive time very well. Just as it cannot tell whether we are doing, or imagining we are doing something, as the example above with the sandstorm showed.

The 5-year projection is an excellent way of taking advantage of these facts. If every day at a deep level of the mind you imagine yourself thinking back over the 'last' 5 years about how well you have controlled your drinking and how much you have personally improved in specific ways you are using both of these facts about the alpha brain wave to your advantage.

Remember whatever we vividly imagine on a repeated basis we come to believe, what we come to believe about ourselves, we tend to act out in our behavior.

So, why specifically 5 years? Psychology has clearly established that any trait or behavior we practice as a part of our lifestyle for 5 years becomes deeply ingrained and durable. A clear case has been made that people who are sober 5 continuous years in AA generally remain that way. Of, course there are exceptions; but the ratio is much in favor of ongoing sobriety from that point on*. The same has been shown with many other things, including weight reduction.

Now imagine how secure, how powerful you would feel if it had already been 5 years and you had been controlling your alcohol well those entire 5 years, plus all of your improved traits had already occurred in full bloom so to speak? How would that feel?

Well now you will experience that. You will lock in that sense of security by integrating your 5-year self into your 'now' self in the exercise and in your dreams.

This will be your final and now daily exercise. You can vary the drinking scenarios after 30 days to be just one of the 3 scenes or all of them as you choose, just make sure to rotate the scenes if you do one at a time.

Do not attempt to skip forward to this exercise until you have done all the rest. Abundant experience has shown that taking this process in the right sequence is critical to its success.

<u>**Do This Exercise for the next 30 days with all 3 scenes of drinking before changing to just one scene. Do this exercise with at least one scene everyday thereafter.**</u>

Use your 10-1 countdown. Go to your ideal place of relaxation. Mentally repeat the following statements to yourself:

Every day I'm getting better and better

Negative thoughts and suggestions no longer influence me

Every day I become more motivated for alcohol moderation and the benefits that brings

Invite your alter ego into your ideal place of relaxation. Now the two of you are feeling much better about one another. Concentrate on the good aspects of your pleasure side. What has it brought to you over the years from childhood on? What do you like about this side of yourself? Now switch perspectives, concentrate on what your responsibility side has done for your pleasure side from childhood on? What does your pleasure side like about the responsibility side of you? Imagine that the two sides of you sit down together and have a conversation like two old friends about anything that comes to mind. After a short time your pleasure side gets up and walks away smiling and you are smiling too.

Now find your movie theater seat in your ideal place, with your movie screen a short distance away. Sit down in the seat and begin to see a set of brief movies in your mind.

On the screen you see your pleasure side in his/her most common drinking setting. Watch as he/she drinks to what is a normal limit (2-3-4 drinks perhaps) then freeze the movie.

Once it is frozen get up from the seat and join your pleasure side on the screen. Walk up to your 'frozen self' and let them know you are there. Say to them that you are ok with them having a good time, but you want to avoid any problems. Ask him/her to stop drinking now.

Sense that your pleasure side is going to cooperate, then un-freeze the movie. Spend the rest of the entire day/night with your pleasure side all the way through to bedtime seeing them not taking any more drinks but feeling good and content.

Now move to a new scene. One that isn't the most common but does happen in your life. Repeat the scenario as before.

Now, change to another scene, this is a special occasion scene. A birthday, holiday, party etc. see your pleasure side drinking slightly more as people tend to on these occasions. Not out of control just a little more. Then repeat the process all the way through to bedtime, remembering to tell your pleasure side you are proud of him or her, they did a great job and reminding as in the prior two scenes to dream they are proud of themselves and enjoying the process. Make sure you imagine yourself doing the same.

Then, after the last scene see you and your pleasure side in the morning both sitting in theater seats watching the screen.

Now move the screen slightly upward and see yourself 5 years in the future. Perceive that this future you is looking back over the last 5 years. He/she is thinking about what a good job they have done being in control of drinking. Your future self is considering why that is and realizes that it is because they did this exercise every single day and took their medication as long as needed, took their supplements as long as they needed, used their CES as long as they needed and still use it occasionally to give their brain a healthy boost.

But more than that has happened. All of your best qualities, those things you like about yourself have gotten stronger and better, while the qualities you don't like about yourself and gotten less and less. Perceive your 5 year future self thinking about what these specific good and less desirable qualities are that have changed.

Now see a beautiful bluish/white light come down and surround the screen, then surround you and your pleasure self as well. Perceive love, peace, power, acceptance and protection from this light.

See your pleasure side smile at you and then get up and step inside you. Concentrate of feeling this part of yourself being there.

Now see the screen come down and your 5 year self step off the screen. Your 5 year self walks up to you and smiles. "I'm proud of you" your 5 year self says and then gently steps inside you. Now you can feel both your pleasure self and your 5 year self-inside you. Welcome the feeling.

Let the light pull away taking the screen with it as it moves quickly off into infinity. Perceive you still feel the love, peace, power, acceptance and protection. See your pleasure side smile at you and then get up and step inside you.

Now count the numbers 1-5 to yourself mentally and open your eyes.

Chapter 18

Loosening The Tool Belt

ReNova is designed to leave you entirely independent of any need for outside supports as you gain mastery of yourself. That will happen best if you begin a gradual process of discontinuing those supports in a staggered fashion. In this way you can judge your readiness without taking risks that could cause setbacks. Judge the results carefully and don't hesitate to reinstate a tool if need be, it won't forever, it just means "not now."

At the end of the 1st 30 days of doing the final exercise, start reducing the number of minutes you use the CES/Alpha Stim. Best to start with using it half the time. Judge this over a period of 2 weeks or so.

- Are you still sleeping well?

- Is your mood still happy relative to actual circumstances or are you becoming anxious, restless or irritable?

- If not, stay with the 30 minutes a day for now. If so, wait another month then try again.

In another month start going to very other day using CES, at two weeks evaluate again. Still good? Then go to twice a week and leave it there and move on to the next tool. At the end of a year you can go to once week. End of 3 years you can safely discontinue if you like.

Now, with a doctors blessing, start to cut back on the Bupropion.

- Take it down 1/3 at a time each 30 days, doing the same evaluation as above but also looking for any change in sex drive or sense of pleasure.

- If all is good, take another 1/3 down each of the next 30 days.

- Then the final 1/3 after that in 30 days. Of course, if you and your doctor determine that is too fast or you start to lose pleasure then discuss that with your doctor and consider going back up again for 30 day cycles before trying again.

- In some rare instances you may find you need to follow your doctor's advice and stay on the Bupropion for some time to come.

Once the Bupropion is fully discontinued, start to cut back on the Brake or other formula you have been taking. Follow the same schedule as with the Bupropion. Your doctor is unlikely to be of a help here, but discussing it with them is never a bad idea. Still, judge yourself for any increased cravings/thoughts/ increased consumption of alcohol and reinstate, if needed. Stay on Brake as long as you need to but, generally most discontinue after no longer than a year. *There is an* important exception to that rule. Those with a strong genetic history of addiction on both sides of their family may want to consider staying on Brake for 3 years.

Again of course with a doctor's advice, most stay on the Naltrexone for 9 months. Then take it every other day until you have been on it for a full year. As with Brake test for increased thoughts/cravings or consumption and reinstate, waiting 3 months before trying again. Same exception applies with a strong genetic history on both sides, with a doctors blessing stay on it 3 years in those cases, then go to every other day to test.

For most, complete independence from supports will be achieved in one year. Always continue the daily visualization exercise, <u>each a day seeing the 5 years being one day later than the day before.</u>

An Afterthought

What can you expect as moderation becomes commonplace for you and the weeks turn into months?

Our experience is that the longer a client remains moderate the less alcohol seems to mean to them. Here are a couple of examples from our case study clients.

First Roger:

A few months after Roger completed ReNova, he and his then fiancé went to a party where everyone was drinking. Upon arrival Roger's fiancé asked him what *he* wanted to drink. He replied "nothing right now." They were at the party for 3 hours. Driving home it occurred to Roger that he hadn't drank at all that night. "Mike, I didn't even think about it the whole time. I mean, *everyone* was drinking all around me and the thought didn't even cross my mind again until after we left. When I did think about it, it wasn't like 'damn I could've been drinking' instead it was more like 'hmmm, ok…well.'

Now Ralph:

"St. Patrick's Day wanna know what I drank? Nothing, not one drop. Just decided I didn't want to drink. First time that has ever happened. And ya know what? It was no big deal at all to me"

Both of these men are formerly heavy, *obsessional* drinkers. The list could go on of examples from others. The point is that ReNova alleviates more than just out of control drinking, anxiety, depression, restlessness and insomnia, it gradually turns alcohol into an after thought.

Can you imagine now how you will feel if you stopped thinking much about alcohol and started thinking more about your life?

Follow these instructions and that is where you will be sooner than you realize.

Freedom awaits you.

How To get More Help

For some this book and the tools and methods it describes will be sufficient to change their lives permanently for the better. If that is the case, we are happy to have helped you. For others working directly with a counselor, knowledgeable with these techniques, will be the preferred method or use of the audio recordings we make available to you.

It is our hope that with the publication about our work, a larger number of professionals' desire to help their clients live more normal lives. We will soon be offering formal training courses to professional addiction counselors and other mental health professionals from around the world. If you want the help of a professional and live outside of the greater Dallas Metroplex area, we advise you to make a counselor of your choice aware of this book and encourage them to contact use after studying this work.

Although the combination of techniques in ReNova is unique, the basic skills and concepts will not be foreign to any well-educated professional counselor/clinician.

Regardless of the way you choose to proceed you will need a medical professional to aid in accessing the medications and CES tools needed for success. You will need Brake or an alternate formula for success.

Remember, ReNova Institute is here to assist with your needs. We offer:

Purchase of Brake Alcohol Reduction support. The most complete formula on the market.

CES Ultra prescription consultation and purchase of a CES at the standard price available everywhere.

Naltrexone/Bupropion medical evaluation and prescription.

Complete ReNova training sessions and audio recordings of each of the exercises contained in this book.

You may visit our website to arrange telemedicine conferences, purchase Brake and the ReNova audio recordings or schedule an initial consultation (free of charge) for in person ReNova training https://www.renovarecoveryinstitute.com.

We wish you the best recovery of your life,

Michael O'Neal, LCDC ADC III

Founder and developer of the ReNova Recovery Method

Mary Burgesser MD

Collaborating physician

How To Convert ReNova To A Sobriety Approach.

Although uncommon, we have experienced clients who could not adapt to moderation successfully. And of course, there are those who simply want to be totally free of alcohol even though they could successfully control their consumption of it. In that event we encourage you change the basic exercise to seeing yourself be happily sober and to use a variation of naltrexone, the long acting injectable drug, Vivitrol.

In the initial commitment development work see yourself doing everything to stay sober and the alternative if you begin to leave off things too quickly. Add a support group and imagine yourself being and feeling good about joining and attending regularly.

In each of the 4 stages of visualization/mind training see yourself in alternate scenarios, doing other fun and/or relaxing things. See yourself with your mind on these activities. Imagine your responsibility self 'stepping' into the scene and 'speaking' to your pleasure side encouraging them to relax and have fun sober. See your responsibility side staying with your pleasure side all the way through to bedtime and follow all other part of the mind training as you would do for moderation, seeing your 5-year self being happy about sobriety. Be sure to add attending your support group to each of the visualizations as well.

We believe that for clients who cannot successfully moderate or want full sobriety a support group is an essential part of recovery. There are many alternatives to AA in today's world if you prefer a different approach and we encourage you to explore several in order to find the best fit.

Make sure however, depending on your circumstances, that you have given moderation a fair shot, or you are very sure in the beginning that moderation is NOT what you want.

Our experience is that it is much easier to convert from trying for moderation to sobriety with this approach than the other way around. So, consider carefully.

About the Author:

Michael O'Neal, LCDC-ADC III is a Licensed and Board
Certified Diplomate Alcohol and Drug Counselor. A 30
year veteran of the profession, Michael has been the
director of 3 different treatment facilities, served a
research coordinator for Texas Christian University @
the Gateway Foundation, been on the curriculum
advisory board of 2 different colleges for the
development of their addiction counseling programs and
taught at the prestigious Institute On Addictions.

A frequent guest lecturer and expert court testimony
provider for recovery advocacy, Michael resides in Dallas
TX., where he was born and raised.

Born addicted, Michael has been in recovery since March 17th, 1986. He now drinks moderately using the ReNova Method he developed.